The Human-AI Partnership:

How AI Can Enhance, Not Replace, Human Potential

SECTION 1:

Introduction – Understanding the Human-AI Partnership

Chapter 1: The Rise of AI: Myths vs. Reality

Introduction

Artificial Intelligence (AI) has been a subject of fascination, excitement, and fear for decades. From sci-fi movies depicting sentient robots taking over the world to news headlines about AI replacing human jobs, public perception of AI is often shaped by exaggerated narratives. However, the reality of AI is far more nuanced. AI is not an all-powerful entity capable of independent thought and emotion but rather a sophisticated tool that enhances human capabilities. In this chapter, we will explore the myths surrounding AI and contrast them with its actual potential and limitations.

Myth 1: AI Will Soon Surpass Human Intelligence and Take Over the World

One of the most common fears surrounding AI is the idea that it will become more intelligent than humans and eventually take control. This notion, often referred to as the "Singularity," suggests that AI will develop self-awareness and make decisions beyond human control.

Reality:

Despite advancements in machine learning and deep learning, AI is still far from achieving general intelligence—the ability to reason, learn from various domains, and apply knowledge in a flexible, human-like way. Current AI systems are "narrow AI," meaning they are designed to perform specific tasks, such as recognizing images, translating languages, or playing chess. They lack true understanding, common sense, and self-awareness. Even the most advanced AI models, like ChatGPT, operate based on statistical probabilities rather than genuine comprehension or independent thought.

Myth 2: AI Thinks and Feels Like Humans

Hollywood often portrays AI as having emotions, consciousness, and even desires. Movies like Her and Ex Machina depict AI developing deep emotional connections with humans, leading to the misconception that AI can experience feelings.

Reality:

AI does not "think" or "feel" in the way humans do. It processes vast amounts of data and identifies patterns, but it lacks emotions, desires, and self-awareness. AI can simulate human conversation and generate text that appears emotional, but this is simply an illusion created by data-driven models. Emotions are deeply tied to human biology, neurotransmitters, and experiences—none of which AI possesses.

Myth 3: AI Will Replace All Human Jobs

One of the biggest concerns about AI is that it will lead to mass unemployment, replacing human workers across industries. Automation in manufacturing, AI-driven customer service, and AI-generated content have raised fears that machines will take over jobs, leaving people without work.

Reality:

While AI is automating some repetitive and data-driven tasks, it is also creating new job opportunities. History has shown that technological advancements often lead to shifts in the job market rather than outright job elimination. For example, the invention of automobiles replaced horse-drawn carriages but created jobs in automobile manufacturing, maintenance, and infrastructure. Similarly, AI is expected to enhance human work by automating routine tasks, allowing professionals to focus on creative, strategic, and decision-making roles. Instead of replacing humans, AI will augment human capabilities and lead to the evolution of the workforce.

Myth 4: AI is Completely Objective and Free from Bias

Many people assume that AI makes decisions based solely on logic and data, free from human biases. The expectation is that AI can serve as an impartial decision-maker in areas like hiring, criminal justice, and finance.

Reality:

AI systems are only as unbiased as the data they are trained on. If the data used to train an AI model contains biases—whether racial, gender-based, or socioeconomic—AI will learn and replicate those biases. There have been documented cases where AI-driven hiring systems favored certain demographics over others or where facial recognition software had higher error rates for specific ethnic groups. To ensure AI systems are fair and ethical, developers must carefully curate training data, apply bias-detection algorithms, and continuously monitor AI behavior.

Myth 5: AI Can Innovate and Create Completely New Ideas on Its Own

AI-generated paintings, poems, and even scientific discoveries have led some to believe that AI can independently innovate and create groundbreaking ideas without human intervention.

Reality:

AI can generate content based on existing data, but it does not possess true creativity or independent thought. Creativity is deeply tied to human experience, emotions, and intuition. AI can assist in the creative process—helping designers brainstorm ideas, aiding scientists in analyzing research data, or composing music based on learned patterns—but it does not have the ability to conceptualize something entirely new without human guidance. Human creativity, curiosity, and critical thinking remain irreplaceable.

The Reality: AI as a Collaborative Tool

Rather than viewing AI as a threat, it should be seen as a tool that enhances human capabilities. AI can assist doctors in diagnosing diseases more accurately, help researchers analyze complex data, and support businesses in making data-driven decisions. However, the human element remains critical in guiding AI, interpreting its results, and ensuring ethical and responsible use.

As AI continues to evolve, it is essential to approach its development with a balanced perspective—embracing its benefits while addressing its challenges. By understanding the myths vs. reality of AI, we can move beyond fear-driven narratives and harness AI's potential to improve society.

Shaping a Future Where AI Enhances, Not Replaces, Humanity

The future of AI is not about machines taking over but about a powerful collaboration between humans and AI. The real question is not whether AI will replace us but how we can leverage AI to amplify human intelligence, creativity, and decision-making. The next chapters will explore how AI can be a valuable partner in various fields, from business and healthcare to education and the arts, paving the way for a future where AI and humanity grow together.

Chapter 2: Humans and Machines – A History of Collaboration

The relationship between humans and machines is not a new phenomenon. For centuries, humans have built and refined machines to extend their physical and mental capabilities. From the invention of the wheel to the rise of artificial intelligence, machines have played a crucial role in shaping civilization. Contrary to popular belief, the integration of machines into daily life has not resulted in human obsolescence but rather in enhanced productivity, creativity, and progress. This chapter explores the historical collaboration between humans and machines, demonstrating how technology has continuously augmented human potential rather than replacing it.

The Early Days: Tools as Extensions of Human Abilities

Human ingenuity has always driven technological progress. The earliest machines were simple tools designed to assist in daily survival. The invention of fire-making tools, stone weapons, and agricultural implements enabled early humans to hunt more effectively, cultivate land, and build permanent settlements.

One of the most significant breakthroughs was the wheel, invented around 3500 BCE. It revolutionized transportation and commerce, allowing humans to move goods and people more efficiently. Similarly, simple machines such as levers, pulleys, and inclined planes helped humans lift heavy objects and construct monumental structures like the Egyptian pyramids.

These early machines did not replace human labor but rather enhanced efficiency and enabled civilizations to expand.

The Industrial Revolution: Machines Transform Society

The Industrial Revolution (18th–19th century) marked a turning point in human-machine collaboration. The invention of steam engines, mechanized looms, and assembly lines dramatically increased productivity in agriculture, textiles, and manufacturing. Factories replaced small-scale manual labor, leading to urbanization and economic growth.

A major fear at the time was that machines would permanently displace workers, much like today's concerns about AI. However, rather than eliminating jobs, the revolution created new industries and employment opportunities. For example, while traditional textile workers faced challenges, new roles emerged in machine maintenance, engineering, and factory management. The printing press, invented by Johannes Gutenberg in the 15th century, revolutionized knowledge dissemination, increasing literacy rates and democratizing information.

This period demonstrated a key pattern: machines changed the nature of work, but human adaptability led to new opportunities.

The 20th Century: Automation and the Rise of Computers

The 20th century saw rapid advancements in automation, electronics, and computing. The invention of electricity led to machines that required less human effort, and mass production techniques (such as Henry Ford's assembly line) made consumer goods widely available.

In the mid-1900s, computers emerged as a new type of machine that could process information at incredible speeds. The development of ENIAC (1946) and later personal computers in the 1980s transformed industries. Many feared that computers would render human workers obsolete, but instead, they became essential tools for business, communication, and creativity.

Key milestones included:

The invention of the transistor (1947) and microprocessor (1971), which led to smaller, faster, and more affordable computers.
The rise of automation in manufacturing, reducing the need for repetitive labor while increasing production efficiency.
The birth of the internet (1960s–1990s), which connected the world and expanded human knowledge-sharing.

While machines took over repetitive and dangerous tasks, they opened new avenues for innovation, entrepreneurship, and global connectivity.

The Digital Age: Artificial Intelligence and Human Enhancement

In the 21st century, artificial intelligence and machine learning have become the next frontier of human-machine collaboration. AI-driven systems assist in healthcare, finance, education, entertainment, and space exploration.

For instance:

Medical AI helps doctors diagnose diseases faster and more accurately.
AI-powered robotics assist in delicate surgeries, reducing human error.
Machine learning in finance predicts market trends and fraud detection.
Smart assistants (like Siri, Alexa, and Google Assistant) enhance everyday convenience.

The fear that AI will replace humans is reminiscent of past concerns about industrial machines and computers. However, history shows that machines enhance human potential rather than diminish it.

Lessons from History: The Future of Human-Machine Collaboration

Looking at history, we can identify recurring patterns:

Machines take over repetitive and dangerous tasks, allowing humans to focus on creativity, problem-solving, and innovation.

Technological progress creates new job opportunities, even as some traditional roles evolve or disappear. Adaptability is key—humans who learn to work with new technologies thrive in changing environments.

The next phase of AI and automation will require ethical considerations, careful governance, and an emphasis on human-AI partnerships. AI is not here to replace human intelligence but to augment it, making us more efficient, creative, and capable.

A Future of Synergy, Not Replacement

From primitive tools to artificial intelligence, human history is a testament to our ability to integrate technology into our lives to solve problems and push boundaries. Machines have always been collaborators rather than competitors in human progress. As AI evolves, it is up to society to embrace it as a tool for empowerment rather than a threat.

Chapter 3: The Philosophy of AI – Partner or Replacement?

Artificial intelligence has rapidly integrated into modern life, shaping industries and influencing daily activities.

From assisting doctors in diagnosing diseases to optimizing logistics and recommending content online, AI has become an indispensable tool. However, a pressing question remains: Is AI merely an advanced assistant, or does it pose a threat to human intelligence and employment?

This chapter explores the philosophical debate surrounding AI's role in society, examining whether it serves as a collaborator that enhances human potential or a force that could replace human ingenuity. By analyzing AI's capabilities and limitations, we aim to establish a balanced perspective on its future impact.

The Dual Narrative of AI: Friend or Foe?

Discussions about AI often fall into two contrasting viewpoints. On one side, AI is seen as an invaluable partner that augments human intelligence, automates tedious tasks, and increases productivity. Proponents argue that AI allows humans to focus on creativity, problem-solving, and complex decision-making.

On the other side, skeptics warn that AI threatens jobs, diminishes human creativity, and could eventually surpass human intelligence. Concerns about mass unemployment, dependency on AI-driven decision-making, and ethical dilemmas regarding automation fuel the fear that AI may not remain a mere assistant but become a replacement.

While both perspectives have merit, history suggests that technological advancements do not eliminate human contributions but rather transform and elevate them.

The Role of AI in Human Progress

Throughout history, revolutionary inventions have disrupted industries while simultaneously creating new opportunities. The printing press did not replace human learning but instead expanded knowledge-sharing. The steam engine mechanized labor but led to industrial growth and new economic sectors. The internet reshaped communication and commerce, generating countless new careers.

AI follows a similar trajectory. It is not a conscious entity but a tool developed to assist humans. While it can automate and optimize processes, human intuition, ethical reasoning, emotional intelligence, and critical thinking remain irreplaceable.

Understanding the Differences: Human Intelligence vs. Artificial Intelligence

Human intelligence and artificial intelligence operate in fundamentally different ways. Humans possess emotional depth, creativity, and ethical reasoning—qualities AI cannot replicate. Human decision-making is influenced by intuition, moral values, and an understanding of abstract concepts. Humans can adapt spontaneously, think critically, and understand complex emotions.

In contrast, AI excels at processing large amounts of data, identifying patterns, and automating repetitive tasks. It can optimize efficiency and increase accuracy in areas such as medical diagnostics, financial forecasting, and manufacturing. However, AI lacks common sense, genuine creativity, emotional intelligence, and ethical judgment. While it can simulate human behavior to an extent, it does not possess independent thought or true understanding.

AI's Strengths: What AI Can Do

AI is most effective in tasks that require data analysis, pattern recognition, and automation. It can analyze massive datasets far beyond human capability, making it invaluable in areas such as medical research, cybersecurity, and climate modeling. AI can also enhance productivity by handling repetitive and time-consuming tasks, allowing professionals to focus on innovation and strategy.

Additionally, AI-powered systems have improved efficiency across industries by reducing errors and enhancing precision. In healthcare, AI-assisted tools help diagnose diseases earlier and more accurately. In business, AI streamlines operations, improving decision-making and customer service.

AI's Limitations: What AI Cannot Do

Despite its capabilities, AI has several inherent limitations. It lacks common sense reasoning, struggling with tasks that require real-world understanding beyond its training data. AI cannot truly comprehend emotions or empathize with human experiences, making it unsuitable for roles that demand deep interpersonal connections.

Another limitation is AI's dependence on data. Since AI systems learn from existing datasets, their outputs are only as good as the information they are trained on. This makes them vulnerable to biases and inaccuracies. Moreover, AI lacks independent ethical reasoning. While it can be programmed with ethical guidelines, it does not possess the ability to make moral judgments like humans do.

Creativity is another domain where AI falls short. While AI can generate content, music, and artwork based on existing patterns, it does not possess true original thought or inspiration. AI-generated works rely on learned styles rather than personal experiences, emotions, or intuition.

The Future: Human-AI Synergy

Rather than viewing AI as a replacement, it is more productive to see it as a collaborative force that enhances human capabilities. Some of the most promising applications of AI involve human-AI partnerships. In medicine, AI aids doctors in diagnosing diseases more accurately, but human expertise is still essential for treatment decisions. In the creative industry, AI assists artists, writers, and musicians, expanding their potential rather than replacing their talents. In business, AI-driven tools support decision-making, but strategic thinking remains a human responsibility.

By fostering a human-led approach, where AI is used as an assistive tool rather than an autonomous decision-maker, we can maximize the benefits of AI while preserving the irreplaceable elements of human intelligence.

AI as an Amplifier, not a Replacement

The debate about AI's role in society is ultimately about how we choose to use it. AI, like all technological advancements, has the potential to both empower and disrupt. However, history shows that innovation tends to enhance human capabilities rather than eliminate them.

The key to a successful future lies in human-AI collaboration. Instead of fearing AI as a rival, we should embrace it as a tool that amplifies human intelligence. By leveraging AI's strengths while recognizing its limitations, we can ensure that AI remains a partner in progress—one that helps humanity reach new heights without diminishing our unique qualities.

Chapter 4: What AI Can and Cannot Do

Artificial Intelligence (AI) has rapidly advanced in recent years, transforming industries, automating tasks, and reshaping how we work and interact with technology. However, despite its incredible capabilities, AI has significant limitations that prevent it from replacing human intelligence entirely. While it excels in data-driven decision-making, automation, and efficiency, it struggles with creativity, emotional intelligence, and ethical reasoning.

This chapter explores what AI can do effectively and where it falls short, providing a clear understanding of AI's true potential and its limitations.

What AI Can Do

1. Process Large Amounts of Data at Unmatched Speed

AI is designed to handle vast amounts of data quickly and efficiently. It can analyze, categorize, and extract insights from datasets that would take humans months or even years to process. For example, AI-driven analytics tools help businesses track market trends, while AI in medicine can analyze millions of patient records to identify patterns in diseases.

2. Automate Repetitive and Routine Tasks

AI is highly effective in automating repetitive, rule-based tasks. This includes:

Automating customer service responses with AI chatbots.
Handling data entry and document processing.
Managing supply chain logistics efficiently.
By reducing human involvement in such tasks, AI helps businesses cut costs and improve efficiency.

3. Recognize Patterns and Make Predictions

AI algorithms are trained to recognize patterns and make accurate predictions. This ability is used in:

Healthcare – AI predicts disease outbreaks and diagnoses illnesses based on symptoms.
Finance – AI detects fraudulent transactions and predicts stock market trends.
Retail – AI recommends products to customers based on purchasing behavior.
This predictive power enables businesses and organizations to make informed decisions.

4. Assist in Scientific and Technological Advancements

AI plays a vital role in scientific research and innovation. It is used to:

Design new drugs and accelerate clinical trials.
Improve weather forecasting and climate modeling.
Enhance space exploration by analyzing astronomical data.

By leveraging AI, scientists and researchers can make discoveries faster and with greater accuracy.

5. Enhance Creativity Through Assistance

While AI does not create original ideas, it assists humans in creative fields. AI can:

Generate music and artwork based on existing styles.
Help writers by suggesting text completions and grammar corrections.
Create AI-generated movie scripts, designs, and visual effects.
However, the final creative input and originality still come from human imagination.

6. Improve Decision-Making and Optimization

AI optimizes processes in multiple industries by analyzing data and recommending the best course of action. Examples include:

In healthcare – AI helps doctors diagnose diseases faster and recommend treatments.
In business – AI analyzes consumer behavior to enhance marketing strategies.
In transportation – AI optimizes traffic management systems to reduce congestion.
While AI provides valuable insights, humans are still responsible for making final decisions.

What AI Cannot Do

1. Understand Emotions and Exhibit True Empathy

AI can mimic emotions through Natural Language Processing (NLP) and facial recognition, but it does not genuinely understand or feel emotions. AI chatbots may respond in a friendly manner, but they lack the ability to experience happiness, sadness, or empathy in the way humans do. This limitation makes AI unsuitable for roles requiring deep emotional intelligence, such as therapy or counseling.

2. Think Independently or Develop Original Ideas

AI operates based on the data it is trained on. It does not possess independent thought, consciousness, or creativity. For example:

AI can generate artwork, but it follows predefined patterns.
AI can write stories, but it lacks real-life experiences or deep emotional depth.
True innovation and original thinking still require human intelligence and imagination.

3. Make Ethical and Moral Decisions

AI lacks the ability to judge morality or understand ethical complexities. AI systems can be programmed with ethical guidelines, but they do not possess a moral compass of their own. This creates challenges in:

Autonomous vehicles – Deciding whom to save in an unavoidable accident.
Hiring processes – Avoiding bias in AI-driven recruitment systems.
Law enforcement – Ensuring AI-driven surveillance respects human rights.
AI lacks the nuanced understanding that humans have when dealing with ethical dilemmas.

4. Exhibit Common Sense and Adapt to Unstructured Situations

Humans rely on common sense to make everyday decisions, something AI struggles with. AI systems work well with structured data but struggle with unpredictable or unstructured situations. For example:

AI might fail to recognize sarcasm or humor in human conversations.
AI-powered robots might struggle to adapt to an unfamiliar environment without precise instructions.
This limitation makes AI unreliable in scenarios that require spontaneous thinking.

5. Replace Human Relationships and Social Interactions

AI can facilitate communication but cannot replace genuine human relationships. While virtual assistants and chatbots simulate conversations, they lack real emotional depth and social awareness. People seek human connection, trust, and emotional bonds that AI simply cannot provide.

6. Function Without Human Supervision

AI requires human oversight to function effectively. It does not possess true autonomy or self-awareness. Without proper training and data input, AI models can make mistakes, show biases, or provide incorrect results.

AI in healthcare must be monitored to avoid misdiagnosing patients.
AI in finance requires regulation to prevent biased decision-making.
AI in security must be supervised to ensure ethical use.
Thus, AI cannot operate independently without human intervention and correction.

The Future of AI in Human Collaboration

AI is a powerful tool, but it is not a substitute for human intelligence, creativity, or ethical reasoning. It excels at processing data, automating tasks, and optimizing decision-making, yet it lacks empathy, common sense, moral judgment, and true originality.

Rather than viewing AI as a replacement, we should embrace it as a partner. The most effective future lies in human-AI collaboration, where AI enhances human productivity while humans provide ethical reasoning, creativity, and emotional intelligence. By understanding what AI can and cannot do, we can use its strengths responsibly while ensuring that human qualities remain at the heart of decision-making and innovation.

Chapter 5: The Human Edge – Why Creativity and Intuition Matter

In an era where Artificial Intelligence (AI) is transforming industries and automating countless tasks, many wonder: What remains uniquely human? While AI can analyze vast amounts of data, predict trends, and even generate content, it lacks two critical qualities that define human intelligence—creativity and intuition. These abilities allow humans to innovate, adapt, and make decisions beyond logic and data.

Creativity fuels artistic expression, scientific breakthroughs, and groundbreaking technological advancements. Intuition, often described as a "gut feeling," enables quick decision-making in uncertain situations where data alone is insufficient. Together, these human qualities form an irreplaceable edge in a world increasingly dominated by AI.

The Power of Human Creativity

1. The Essence of Creativity

Creativity is the ability to generate new ideas, solutions, and artistic expressions. Unlike AI, which relies on existing data, humans create something truly original. Creativity is not just about art—it drives innovation in every field, from science to business.

Examples of human-driven creativity include:

Albert Einstein's theory of relativity, which changed our understanding of space and time.
Leonardo da Vinci's inventions, which were ahead of their time.
Steve Jobs' vision for Apple, which revolutionized personal technology.

These breakthroughs required imagination, intuition, and insight; qualities AI cannot replicate.

2. AI's Role in Creative Assistance

AI can support creativity but does not replace it. For example:

AI-generated art is based on analyzing existing styles rather than true originality.
AI-powered music composition tools remix past compositions rather than creating new genres.
AI writing assistants suggest words but lack the depth of human storytelling.

While AI augments creativity, it is humans who inject meaning, originality, and emotional depth into their creations.

3. Why AI Struggles with True Creativity

AI lacks experiences, emotions, and independent thought—key ingredients of creativity. Human creativity comes from:

Personal experiences that shape unique perspectives.
Emotions and storytelling that resonate with others.
Trial and error, leading to unexpected discoveries.

AI, on the other hand, follows predefined algorithms and cannot think outside the data it is trained on.

The Role of Human Intuition

1. What is Intuition?

Intuition is the ability to understand something instantly without conscious reasoning. It is often referred to as a "gut feeling" or an "inner voice" that guides decision-making. Intuition comes from experience, pattern recognition, and subconscious processing.

For example, an experienced doctor might sense a patient's condition before test results confirm it. A chess grandmaster may make a brilliant move based on instinct rather than deep calculation. Business leaders often take risks based on intuition rather than numbers alone.

2. Why Intuition Matters in Decision-Making

AI relies solely on data to make decisions, whereas humans blend logic with intuition to navigate complex situations. Intuition plays a crucial role in:

Leadership – Successful leaders often rely on gut instinct to make bold decisions.
Negotiations – Intuitive people can sense emotions and respond accordingly.
Crisis management – In unpredictable situations, intuition helps make quick choices when data is incomplete.

AI struggles in these areas because it lacks an inherent understanding of human emotions, ethics, and unpredictable variables.

3. The Limits of AI in Intuitive Thinking

While AI can analyze patterns, it does not possess intuition because:

It lacks real-world experiences that shape human judgment.
It cannot process emotions or gut feelings.
It is dependent on existing data and cannot make instinctive leaps.

For example, AI may suggest the best financial investment based on past trends, but a skilled investor might sense an unpredictable market shift that AI overlooks.

The Future: Humans and AI as Partners, Not Replacements

Instead of fearing AI as a replacement for human intelligence, we should see it as a tool that enhances human creativity and intuition. The most successful innovations will come from human-AI collaboration, where AI handles data-driven tasks while humans provide insight, originality, and emotional intelligence.

How to Leverage AI While Retaining the Human Edge

Use AI to automate repetitive tasks, freeing up time for creative thinking.
Allow AI to assist in idea generation, but rely on humans for final creative direction.
Trust human intuition for decision-making in ambiguous situations where AI lacks depth.

The future belongs to those who can merge AI's efficiency with human ingenuity. While AI can refine and enhance human efforts, it is creativity and intuition that will continue to shape the world in ways AI never can.

As AI continues to evolve, the human edge remains essential. Creativity fuels progress, and intuition guides decision-making beyond logic and data. While AI can assist, it cannot replace the human spirit—our ability to imagine, feel, and take risks.

Rather than fearing AI's rise, we should embrace it as a partner in our journey toward greater innovation. By blending human ingenuity with AI's capabilities, we can unlock limitless possibilities—but only if we recognize and preserve what makes us truly human.

SECTION 2: AI as an Amplifier of Human Intelligence

Chapter 6: The Cognitive Augmentation of Humans by AI

Artificial Intelligence (AI) is not just about automation—it is also about enhancing human cognitive abilities. While some fear AI will replace human intelligence, the reality is that AI has the power to augment our cognitive functions, making us smarter, faster, and more efficient. From improving decision-making to enhancing memory and problem-solving, AI is becoming an extension of the human mind.

In this chapter, we will explore how AI amplifies human intelligence, the ways it enhances our thinking, learning, and problem-solving abilities, and the ethical considerations that come with this transformation.

How AI Enhances Human Cognition

AI augments human intelligence by processing vast amounts of information, detecting patterns, and offering insights that would take humans much longer to uncover. Unlike automation, which simply replaces tasks, cognitive augmentation strengthens human abilities, making us more productive and insightful.

1. AI as an Extension of Human Memory

One of AI's most powerful functions is its ability to store, retrieve, and organize vast amounts of data, effectively acting as an extension of human memory.

Medical professionals use AI to store patient records, analyze symptoms, and recall treatment histories. Researchers rely on AI to scan thousands of studies in seconds, extracting key insights.
Students and professionals benefit from AI-powered note-taking tools that summarize information efficiently.

While the human brain has limitations in storing and recalling precise details, AI provides instant access to relevant knowledge, reducing cognitive overload and improving productivity.

2. AI-Driven Decision-Making and Problem-Solving

AI systems are excellent at analyzing complex data, identifying patterns, and making recommendations. This has transformed decision-making in various fields:

In business, AI helps executives predict market trends, optimize supply chains, and identify risks.

In healthcare, AI aids in diagnosing diseases, recommending treatments, and predicting patient outcomes.
In finance, AI-driven systems detect fraudulent transactions and guide investment strategies.

While AI provides data-driven insights, human intuition and ethical considerations are still essential in making the final decisions.

3. AI-Powered Learning and Skill Development

AI has revolutionized education and skill acquisition, making learning more personalized and efficient.

Adaptive learning platforms analyze students' strengths and weaknesses, tailoring lessons accordingly.
Language learning apps use AI to provide real-time feedback and pronunciation corrections.
AI tutors and chatbots help students with problem-solving in subjects like math and science.

By accelerating learning and providing customized educational experiences, AI enables people to acquire knowledge and skills faster than ever before.

The Symbiosis of AI and Human Intelligence

Rather than replacing human intelligence, AI creates a collaborative intelligence model, where humans and machines complement each other's strengths.

1. AI's Strengths vs. Human Strengths

AI excels at:

Processing large amounts of data quickly.
Recognizing patterns and trends.
Performing repetitive and precision-based tasks.

Humans excel at:

Creativity, intuition, and emotional intelligence.
Ethical decision-making and critical thinking.
Understanding abstract concepts and moral dilemmas.

By working together, AI and humans enhance each other's abilities, leading to better outcomes in every industry.

2. Human-AI Collaboration in the Workplace

AI is transforming industries by enhancing human productivity rather than replacing jobs.

Lawyers use AI for legal research, allowing them to focus on strategy and argumentation.

Doctors leverage AI diagnostics, but their expertise is needed for personalized patient care.
Artists and designers use AI tools to enhance creativity but remain the core creative force.

The best results come from a balance between human intelligence and AI capabilities, ensuring efficiency while maintaining the human touch.

Ethical Considerations and Challenges

As AI becomes deeply integrated into human cognition, ethical questions arise.

1. Dependency on AI

With AI handling more cognitive tasks, there is a risk of humans becoming too dependent on it. If AI systems fail, do we have the ability to function without them?

2. Privacy and Data Security

AI-powered cognitive tools collect vast amounts of personal data. Ensuring privacy, security, and ethical data usage is crucial.

3. Bias in AI Decision-Making

AI systems are only as unbiased as the data they are trained on. Ensuring fairness in AI-assisted decision-making is essential to avoid discrimination.

AI is not a competitor to human intelligence, but an amplifier that enhances our cognitive abilities. From improving memory and learning to aiding decision-making and creativity, AI acts as an extension of the human mind. However, responsible use, ethical considerations, and maintaining a balance between human intuition and AI-driven insights are crucial.

The future belongs to those who embrace AI not as a replacement, but as a partner—enhancing intelligence, empowering innovation, and expanding human potential like never before.

Chapter 6: The Cognitive Augmentation of Humans by AI

Artificial Intelligence (AI) is not just about automation—it is also about enhancing human cognitive abilities. While some fear AI will replace human intelligence, the reality is that AI has the power to augment our cognitive functions, making us smarter, faster, and more efficient. From improving decision-making to enhancing memory and problem-solving, AI is becoming an extension of the human mind.

In this chapter, we will explore how AI amplifies human intelligence, the ways it enhances our thinking, learning, and problem-solving abilities, and the ethical considerations that come with this transformation.

How AI Enhances Human Cognition

AI augments human intelligence by processing vast amounts of information, detecting patterns, and offering insights that would take humans much longer to uncover. Unlike automation, which simply replaces tasks, cognitive augmentation strengthens human abilities, making us more productive and insightful.

1. AI as an Extension of Human Memory

One of AI's most powerful functions is its ability to store, retrieve, and organize vast amounts of data, effectively acting as an extension of human memory.

Medical professionals use AI to store patient records, analyze symptoms, and recall treatment histories.

Researchers rely on AI to scan thousands of studies in seconds, extracting key insights.
Students and professionals benefit from AI-powered note-taking tools that summarize information efficiently.

While the human brain has limitations in storing and recalling precise details, AI provides instant access to relevant knowledge, reducing cognitive overload and improving productivity.

2. AI-Driven Decision-Making and Problem-Solving

AI systems are excellent at analyzing complex data, identifying patterns, and making recommendations. This has transformed decision-making in various fields:

In business, AI helps executives predict market trends, optimize supply chains, and identify risks.
In healthcare, AI aids in diagnosing diseases, recommending treatments, and predicting patient outcomes.
In finance, AI-driven systems detect fraudulent transactions and guide investment strategies.

While AI provides data-driven insights, human intuition and ethical considerations are still essential in making the final decisions.

3. AI-Powered Learning and Skill Development

AI has revolutionized education and skill acquisition, making learning more personalized and efficient.

Adaptive learning platforms analyze students' strengths and weaknesses, tailoring lessons accordingly.
Language learning apps use AI to provide real-time feedback and pronunciation corrections.
AI tutors and chatbots help students with problem-solving in subjects like math and science.

By accelerating learning and providing customized educational experiences, AI enables people to acquire knowledge and skills faster than ever before.

The Symbiosis of AI and Human Intelligence

Rather than replacing human intelligence, AI creates a collaborative intelligence model, where humans and machines complement each other's strengths.

1. AI's Strengths vs. Human Strengths

AI excels at:

Processing large amounts of data quickly.
Recognizing patterns and trends.
Performing repetitive and precision-based tasks.

Humans excel at:

Creativity, intuition, and emotional intelligence.
Ethical decision-making and critical thinking.
Understanding abstract concepts and moral dilemmas.

By working together, AI and humans enhance each other's abilities, leading to better outcomes in every industry.

2. Human-AI Collaboration in the Workplace

AI is transforming industries by enhancing human productivity rather than replacing jobs.

Lawyers use AI for legal research, allowing them to focus on strategy and argumentation.
Doctors leverage AI diagnostics, but their expertise is needed for personalized patient care.
Artists and designers use AI tools to enhance creativity but remain the core creative force.

The best results come from a balance between human intelligence and AI capabilities, ensuring efficiency while maintaining the human touch.

Ethical Considerations and Challenges

As AI becomes deeply integrated into human cognition, ethical questions arise.

1. Dependency on AI

With AI handling more cognitive tasks, there is a risk of humans becoming too dependent on it. If AI systems fail, do we have the ability to function without them?

2. Privacy and Data Security

AI-powered cognitive tools collect vast amounts of personal data. Ensuring privacy, security, and ethical data usage is crucial.

3. Bias in AI Decision-Making

AI systems are only as unbiased as the data they are trained on. Ensuring fairness in AI-assisted decision-making is essential to avoid discrimination.

AI is not a competitor to human intelligence, but an amplifier that enhances our cognitive abilities. From improving memory and learning to aiding decision-making and creativity, AI acts as an extension of the human mind. However, responsible use, ethical considerations, and maintaining a balance between human intuition and AI-driven insights are crucial.

The future belongs to those who embrace AI not as a replacement, but as a partner—enhancing intelligence, empowering innovation, and expanding human potential like never before.

Chapter 7: AI and Human Memory Enhancement

Memory is one of the most fundamental aspects of human cognition. It shapes our identities, allows us to learn from past experiences, and helps us make informed decisions. However, human memory is imperfect—we forget things, misremember details, and struggle with information overload.

AI, on the other hand, has the ability to store, organize, and retrieve vast amounts of data with precision. With advancements in artificial intelligence, we are witnessing the emergence of AI-powered memory augmentation, where machines help us retain and recall information more effectively. In this chapter, we explore how AI enhances human memory, the implications of relying on AI for recollection, and the ethical considerations surrounding memory augmentation.

The Nature of Human Memory

Before delving into AI's role, it is important to understand how human memory functions.

Human memory operates in three stages:

Encoding – The process of converting sensory input into meaningful information.
Storage – Retaining information over time.
Retrieval – Accessing stored memories when needed.

However, human memory is:

Fallible – People forget, distort, or misinterpret memories.
Limited in capacity – We cannot remember everything we experience.
Subject to bias – Our emotions and perspectives shape how we recall events.

AI can assist in overcoming these limitations, serving as an external memory system that enhances our cognitive abilities.

How AI Enhances Human Memory

1. AI as an External Storage System

AI-powered devices act as external memory banks, storing and organizing vast amounts of information that we can access anytime.

Smart assistants (e.g., Siri, Google Assistant, Alexa) remember schedules, reminders, and past interactions.
Cloud storage and AI-powered databases allow instant retrieval of documents, notes, and multimedia files.
AI-driven note-taking apps (e.g., Evernote, Notion, Roam Research) categorize and summarize information efficiently.

By offloading memory tasks to AI, humans free up cognitive resources for more complex thinking.

2. AI-Powered Reminders and Recall Systems

One of the most immediate ways AI enhances memory is through intelligent reminders and predictive suggestions.

Smart calendars and AI-driven scheduling apps remind users of appointments, birthdays, and deadlines.
Wearable AI devices track habits, reminding users to exercise, take medication, or drink water.

AI-enhanced search functions help users find old emails, messages, or documents quickly.

These AI systems optimize memory recall, ensuring we never forget important tasks or events.

3. AI and Memory Reinforcement in Learning

AI is revolutionizing education by enhancing memory retention through personalized learning techniques.

Adaptive learning platforms analyze students' weaknesses and reinforce difficult concepts.
AI-powered flashcard apps (e.g., Anki, Quizlet) use spaced repetition algorithms to help students retain information for longer periods.
Voice assistants and chatbots provide on-demand explanations, reinforcing learning through repetition.

By customizing the learning experience, AI improves knowledge retention and recall.

4. AI in Memory Rehabilitation for Cognitive Disorders

AI is making groundbreaking contributions to memory restoration and cognitive rehabilitation for individuals suffering from memory-related conditions.

AI-powered apps (e.g., ReMind, Clevermind) assist people with Alzheimer's and dementia by providing memory cues.

AI-driven brain implants and neuroprosthetics are being developed to enhance memory in patients with neurological disorders.
Chatbots and virtual assistants help elderly individuals recall past events, recognize faces, and navigate daily routines.

By acting as a memory aid, AI improves the quality of life for individuals with cognitive impairments.

The Potential Risks of AI-Enhanced Memory

While AI offers numerous advantages in memory augmentation, it also poses several risks:

1. Over-Reliance on AI

With AI handling memory tasks, humans may become too dependent, leading to cognitive decline. If AI systems fail, individuals may struggle to recall essential information.

2. Privacy and Data Security Concerns

AI-enhanced memory systems store vast amounts of personal and sensitive data. If this data is hacked or misused, it could lead to identity theft, surveillance, or manipulation.

3. Ethical Implications of Memory Manipulation

AI-powered memory tools could be used to alter, distort, or erase memories, raising ethical concerns. If AI controls what people remember, it could be exploited for misinformation or social engineering.

4. Loss of Natural Recall Abilities

The more we rely on AI for memory, the less we exercise our natural ability to recall information. This could impact creativity, intuition, and independent thinking.

Striking a Balance: The Future of AI and Human Memory

To maximize the benefits of AI-enhanced memory while minimizing risks, we must adopt a balanced approach:

Use AI as a tool, not a crutch – AI should enhance, not replace, our cognitive functions.
Prioritize data security – Strong regulations must protect users' privacy and prevent memory manipulation.
Encourage natural memory exercises – Cognitive training, mindfulness, and traditional memory techniques should be used alongside AI.

Develop ethical AI frameworks – AI memory tools should be designed to uphold transparency and user control.

AI is transforming human memory, making it more efficient, organized, and accessible. Whether through intelligent reminders, enhanced learning, or cognitive rehabilitation, AI is bridging the gap between human forgetfulness and machine precision.

However, as we embrace AI-powered memory augmentation, we must remain vigilant about ethical concerns and ensure that AI serves as a supportive partner rather than a replacement for natural cognition. The future of human memory lies not in surrendering our ability to remember, but in harmonizing our minds with intelligent technology, creating a world where humans and AI work together to preserve knowledge, enhance intelligence, and push the boundaries of memory.

Chapter 8: AI in Decision-Making: Strengthening Human Judgment

Decision-making is at the heart of human progress. Whether in business, healthcare, finance, governance, or personal life, making the right decisions at the right time can be the difference between success and failure. Traditionally, human judgment has relied on experience, intuition, and reasoning, but with the advent of artificial intelligence, decision-making is undergoing a transformative shift.

AI has the power to process vast amounts of data, recognize patterns, and provide insights that humans might overlook. However, rather than replacing human judgment, AI serves as a powerful augmentation tool, strengthening our ability to make better, faster, and more informed decisions. This chapter explores how AI enhances human decision-making, its benefits and risks, and the ethical considerations that come with AI-assisted choices.

The Evolution of Decision-Making: From Instinct to Intelligence

Throughout history, decision-making has evolved in three key phases:

Instinct-Based Decisions – Early humans relied on gut feelings and survival instincts to make choices. Data-Driven Decisions – With the advent of science, humans started basing decisions on facts, statistics, and analysis rather than pure intuition.

AI-Augmented Decisions – Today, AI assists in making complex decisions by processing big data, machine learning models, and predictive analytics.

While humans bring creativity, moral reasoning, and contextual understanding to decision-making, AI adds efficiency, precision, and speed—leading to a powerful synergy.

How AI Strengthens Human Judgment

1. AI for Data Analysis and Pattern Recognition

AI can analyze massive datasets far beyond human capacity, identifying hidden patterns and correlations that might otherwise go unnoticed.

In finance, AI predicts market trends and helps investors make informed trading decisions.
In healthcare, AI analyzes patient records to assist doctors in diagnosing diseases earlier and more accurately.
In law enforcement, AI scans crime data to predict potential security threats.

By providing data-driven insights, AI enhances human ability to interpret complex situations and make better decisions.

2. AI for Risk Assessment and Prediction

AI-powered predictive analytics help individuals and organizations anticipate potential risks and opportunities before they arise.

In business, AI forecasts market demand, helping companies adjust strategies proactively.
In disaster management, AI models predict natural disasters, enabling better preparedness.
In cybersecurity, AI detects fraud and cyber threats before they escalate.

By assessing risks with greater accuracy, AI strengthens human judgment, allowing for more strategic decision-making.

3. AI as a Decision Support System

AI functions as a decision support tool, offering recommendations but leaving the final decision to humans.

In healthcare, AI suggests treatment options, but doctors make the final call.
In customer service, AI chatbots assist agents by suggesting responses, but humans handle complex issues.
In aviation, autopilot assists pilots but does not replace their expertise.

AI ensures informed decision-making while preserving human oversight.

4. AI for Removing Bias in Decision-Making

Human decisions are often affected by cognitive biases, such as confirmation bias or emotional influence. AI, when properly designed, can provide objective, data-driven recommendations that reduce human bias.

In hiring, AI screens job applications without bias toward gender, ethnicity, or age.
In loan approvals, AI evaluates applicants based on financial data rather than subjective impressions.
In judicial systems, AI analyzes legal precedents to help judges make fairer rulings.

While AI can minimize bias, it must be carefully monitored to ensure it does not inherit biases from its training data.

5. AI for Faster Decision-Making

In high-pressure environments, speed is crucial. AI can process information in real-time, allowing humans to act quickly and decisively.

In emergency response, AI predicts the fastest routes for ambulances and fire trucks.

In stock trading, AI algorithms make split-second investment decisions.
In manufacturing, AI detects defects in real-time, preventing costly delays.

By reducing decision fatigue and expediting analysis, AI enables humans to focus on strategic thinking rather than being bogged down by data processing.

Challenges and Ethical Considerations in AI-Driven Decision-Making

While AI enhances decision-making, it also introduces challenges that require careful consideration:

1. The Risk of Over-Reliance on AI

As AI becomes more sophisticated, there is a risk that humans may over-depend on machine-generated insights without questioning them. Blind trust in AI could lead to errors, especially when AI models encounter unforeseen situations.

2. Algorithmic Bias and Fairness

AI systems learn from historical data, which may contain biases. If unchecked, AI could reinforce societal inequalities rather than eliminate them.

For example:

AI-driven hiring systems could unintentionally discriminate against underrepresented groups.
AI used in criminal justice could disproportionately target certain demographics.

To prevent this, AI models must be continuously audited for fairness and transparency.

3. Human Accountability and AI Decisions

Who is responsible when an AI-assisted decision goes wrong? In critical sectors like medicine, finance, and law enforcement, accountability must be clearly defined.

Ethical frameworks must ensure:

AI serves as a support tool, not the sole decision-maker.
Humans remain in control and can override AI when necessary.
AI-driven decisions are explainable and transparent.

4. Privacy and Data Security Concerns

AI decision-making relies on massive amounts of personal and sensitive data. If mishandled, this data could be exposed, leading to privacy violations and cyber threats.

Stricter data protection regulations are needed to safeguard personal information.
AI models should be designed with data minimization principles to avoid unnecessary data collection.

Balancing innovation with privacy is crucial for ethical AI implementation.

Striking the Right Balance: AI and Human Judgment as Partners

To ensure AI enhances human decision-making rather than replacing it, we must focus on collaborative intelligence:

AI should assist, not dictate – Humans must always have the final say in critical decisions.
Continuous human oversight is essential – AI models should be monitored to prevent bias, errors, and ethical breaches.
AI training should include ethical considerations – Developers must design AI systems that prioritize fairness, transparency, and accountability.
Public awareness and AI literacy – People should be educated on how AI makes decisions, enabling them to question and challenge AI outputs when necessary.

When used responsibly, AI can act as an enhancer of human judgment, providing valuable insights while leaving moral, ethical, and creative reasoning to humans.

AI is not here to replace human decision-making but to amplify our ability to make better choices. From healthcare and finance to business and security, AI-driven insights provide unparalleled precision, efficiency, and speed. However, human intuition, ethics, and contextual understanding remain irreplaceable.

The future lies in a symbiotic partnership, where AI handles data-heavy analysis, and humans apply wisdom, creativity, and moral reasoning to make final decisions. By leveraging AI as a tool rather than a replacement, we can create a future where machines empower humans to make the best decisions possible, shaping a smarter and more responsible world.

Chapter 9: How AI Helps Us Process Complex Data

In today's world, data is growing at an exponential rate. Every second, trillions of bytes of information are generated from businesses, social media, healthcare, science, and countless other domains. However, raw data alone is meaningless unless it can be processed, analyzed, and interpreted effectively.

This is where Artificial Intelligence (AI) revolutionizes data processing. AI can identify patterns, extract insights, and predict outcomes at a speed and scale that far surpass human capability. It enables businesses to make data-driven decisions, helps scientists uncover breakthroughs, and empowers individuals with personalized recommendations.

In this chapter, we will explore how AI processes complex data, its applications across industries, and the challenges that come with AI-driven data analysis.

The Explosion of Complex Data

Before AI, data processing was mostly manual or rule-based, making it difficult to analyze large datasets efficiently. However, in today's digital age, the sheer volume, variety, and velocity of data make traditional methods ineffective.

1. The Three Vs of Big Data

Volume – Enormous amounts of data are generated daily from businesses, social media, and sensors.
Variety – Data exists in many formats, such as text, images, videos, and numerical datasets.
Velocity – Data is produced at an unprecedented speed, requiring real-time processing.

AI's ability to handle big data makes it an invaluable tool in transforming unstructured information into meaningful insights.

How AI Processes Complex Data

1. Data Collection and Preprocessing

Raw data is often incomplete, unstructured, or noisy. AI helps clean and organize it through:

Automated Data Cleaning – AI removes errors, duplicates, and inconsistencies in datasets.
Data Structuring – AI converts unstructured data (e.g., social media posts) into analyzable formats.
Missing Data Handling – AI predicts missing values based on available data patterns.

This preprocessing ensures that data is accurate and ready for meaningful analysis.

2. Pattern Recognition and Machine Learning

AI uses machine learning algorithms to detect hidden patterns and trends in massive datasets.

In finance, AI predicts stock market movements based on past data.
In medicine, AI recognizes disease patterns in medical images.
In business, AI identifies customer preferences, helping companies tailor products.

By recognizing patterns beyond human capability, AI transforms complex data into actionable knowledge.

3. Predictive Analytics and Forecasting

AI-powered predictive models analyze historical data to make future projections.

In weather forecasting, AI predicts hurricanes and climate patterns.
In supply chain management, AI anticipates demand fluctuations to optimize inventory.
In healthcare, AI forecasts disease outbreaks based on global health records.

Predictive analytics allows for proactive decision-making, preventing losses and improving efficiency.

4. Natural Language Processing (NLP) for Text Data

Much of today's data exists in text form—emails, reports, articles, and social media conversations. AI-powered Natural Language Processing (NLP) enables machines to understand and analyze human language.

Sentiment Analysis – AI determines public opinion on brands, political issues, or social movements.
Legal Document Analysis – AI scans legal contracts for risks or inconsistencies.
Chatbots and Virtual Assistants – AI processes and responds to customer inquiries automatically.

NLP helps businesses gain insights from textual data, improving customer service and decision-making.

5. Computer Vision for Image and Video Data

Images and videos contain massive amounts of data that AI can process in real-time.

In healthcare, AI analyzes X-rays, MRIs, and CT scans to detect diseases early.
In security, AI-powered facial recognition enhances safety in airports and public places.
In manufacturing, AI detects defects in products to ensure quality control.

AI's ability to process visual data enables automation in numerous industries.

6. Real-Time Data Processing

Some industries require instant analysis of data. AI-powered systems process real-time data streams for immediate action.

Self-Driving Cars – AI interprets traffic conditions and obstacles in real-time.
Stock Trading – AI algorithms make split-second trading decisions based on market trends.
Smart Cities – AI manages traffic signals, energy usage, and emergency response in urban areas.

Real-time AI processing improves efficiency, safety, and decision-making in critical environments.

Applications of AI in Complex Data Processing

1. Healthcare and Medical Research

AI processes vast amounts of genetic, clinical, and pharmaceutical data to:

Detect diseases earlier and more accurately.
Personalize treatments based on a patient's genetic profile.
Speed up drug discovery by simulating chemical reactions.

2. Finance and Banking

AI analyzes financial data to:

Detect fraudulent transactions in milliseconds.
Optimize stock market trading strategies.
Assess customer risk for loans and credit approvals.

3. Business Intelligence and Marketing

AI processes customer behavior data to:

Predict shopping trends and personalize
recommendations.
Optimize advertising campaigns for higher ROI.
Automate customer sentiment analysis for better
branding.

4. Scientific Research and Space Exploration

AI processes massive datasets from:

Telescopes and satellites to map distant galaxies.
Particle physics experiments (e.g., Large Hadron
Collider) to uncover fundamental particles.
Climate studies to track global warming trends.

5. Government and Security

AI helps process national security intelligence to:

Detect cyber threats and prevent attacks.
Monitor suspicious activities through surveillance data.
Predict potential conflicts based on geopolitical trends.

Challenges and Ethical Considerations

1. Data Privacy and Security Risks

AI relies on vast amounts of personal data, raising
concerns about privacy violations.
Cybercriminals can exploit AI systems to manipulate
financial markets or conduct fraud.

2. Algorithmic Bias and Fairness

AI systems learn from historical data, which may
contain biases.
Unfair AI decisions can lead to discriminatory hiring,
credit denial, or wrongful arrests.

3. The Black Box Problem

Many AI models function as black boxes, meaning their
decision-making process is not transparent.
Without interpretability, humans may struggle to trust
AI-driven insights.

The Future of AI in Data Processing

Looking ahead, AI will continue to revolutionize how we process data. Future advancements include:

Explainable AI (XAI) – Making AI decisions more transparent and understandable.
Quantum AI – Using quantum computing to process data even faster.
Edge AI – AI models operating on local devices rather than centralized servers for real-time decisions.

The ultimate goal is to create AI systems that are accurate, fair, secure, and ethically responsible.

AI has transformed data processing from a manual, time-consuming task into an automated, efficient, and highly accurate process. Whether in healthcare, finance, business, or security, AI enables humans to analyze complex data and make informed, data-driven decisions.

However, the power of AI must be used responsibly. As AI-driven data analysis continues to evolve, ethics, transparency, and accountability must remain at the forefront. By leveraging AI as a tool rather than a replacement, we can harness its power to build a smarter, safer, and more insightful world.

Chapter 10:

Emotional Intelligence: A Human Strength AI Cannot Replicate

Artificial Intelligence (AI) has made incredible strides in recent years, outperforming humans in various fields such as data analysis, pattern recognition, and automation. However, despite its computational power, AI lacks a crucial element that defines human interactions—Emotional Intelligence (EI).

Emotional Intelligence, often referred to as EQ (Emotional Quotient), encompasses the ability to recognize, understand, and manage emotions—both in oneself and in others. It plays a vital role in relationships, leadership, decision-making, empathy, and ethical behavior. Unlike AI, which operates based on algorithms and data, humans rely on emotions, intuition, and experience to navigate complex social interactions.

In this chapter, we will explore what Emotional Intelligence is, why it is essential, and why AI, despite its advancements, cannot replicate true human emotions and empathy.

What Is Emotional Intelligence?

Emotional Intelligence is the ability to:

Recognize emotions in oneself and others.
Regulate emotions effectively, especially in stressful situations.
Empathize with others' feelings and perspectives.
Use emotions to enhance decision-making and problem-solving.
Build and maintain social relationships based on trust and understanding.

Renowned psychologist Daniel Goleman identified five key components of Emotional Intelligence:

Self-Awareness – The ability to understand one's own emotions and their impact.
Self-Regulation – The ability to control emotions and adapt to changing situations.
Motivation – The drive to achieve goals despite setbacks.
Empathy – The capacity to understand and share the feelings of others.
Social Skills – The ability to manage relationships and communicate effectively.

These skills are deeply human and contribute to our ability to connect, inspire, and lead in ways AI simply cannot.

Why Emotional Intelligence Matters

1. Human Relationships and Social Interactions

Human interactions are not based solely on logic and facts. They involve nuances, unspoken cues, and emotional depth. For example:

A teacher understands when a student is struggling emotionally, even if their grades do not show it.
A doctor provides not just a diagnosis but also compassion and reassurance to a patient.
A leader motivates employees by acknowledging their emotions and inspiring them.

AI may assist in analyzing data, but it cannot form genuine emotional bonds or interpret human emotions with depth.

2. Decision-Making in High-Stakes Situations

While AI can process massive amounts of information to assist in decision-making, it lacks human intuition. Many critical decisions require a balance between logic and emotion.

For example:

In healthcare, a doctor may decide not to disclose a terminal illness diagnosis in a harsh way, considering the patient's emotional state.
In law enforcement, an officer may use discretion instead of rigidly following automated guidelines.
In business, a manager may prioritize team morale over short-term profits.

AI lacks contextual awareness and moral reasoning, making it unsuitable for decisions requiring empathy.

3. The Role of Empathy in Leadership

Great leaders possess high Emotional Intelligence. They understand what motivates their team, how to resolve conflicts, and how to inspire loyalty and trust.

Empathy allows leaders to:

Recognize when employees are stressed and offer support.
Encourage innovation by fostering an emotionally safe workplace.
Build long-term relationships based on mutual respect and understanding.

AI-powered chatbots and virtual assistants may simulate understanding, but they lack genuine emotional depth required for effective leadership.

Why AI Cannot Replicate Emotional Intelligence

1. AI Lacks True Self-Awareness

Self-awareness is the foundation of Emotional Intelligence. Humans reflect on their emotions, question their decisions, and grow from experiences.

AI, on the other hand, follows programmed rules and learns from data, but it does not "feel" or introspect. It cannot experience:

Regret
Joy
Guilt
Personal growth

Without self-awareness, AI cannot genuinely comprehend emotions, only recognize them based on patterns.

2. AI Can Recognize Emotions, But Not Truly Understand Them

AI-driven emotion recognition software can analyze facial expressions, voice tone, and text sentiment, but this does not mean AI understands emotions.

For example, AI can:

Detect a smiling face, but it does not understand the meaning behind the smile.
Analyze words in a conversation, but it does not grasp sarcasm, cultural context, or deep emotional nuances.

AI mimics emotions without experiencing them, making its responses mechanical rather than heartfelt.

3. AI Lacks the Ability to Form Deep Emotional Bonds

Humans form connections through shared experiences, vulnerability, and mutual understanding. AI, however, is incapable of:

Feeling genuine concern for someone's well-being.
Understanding personal hardships beyond data analysis.
Offering meaningful emotional support beyond scripted responses.

This is why therapy, counseling, and personal mentoring cannot be effectively replaced by AI.

4. AI Cannot Make Ethical or Moral Judgments Based on Emotion

Many human decisions require an emotional and ethical component. AI can calculate the most efficient solution, but it cannot weigh human emotions in ethical dilemmas.

For example:

Should an autonomous car prioritize the lives of passengers or pedestrians in an unavoidable crash?
Should a hiring algorithm consider an applicant's difficult personal circumstances?
Should a military AI system determine when to use force?

AI lacks the moral reasoning and emotional depth required to make such ethical decisions.

The Future: AI as a Tool, Not a Replacement

While AI enhances many aspects of our lives, it is not a substitute for Emotional Intelligence. Instead, AI should be seen as a tool that complements human strengths.

AI can assist therapists, but it cannot replace the human connection in mental health care.
AI can analyze customer sentiment, but it cannot replace human-led conflict resolution.
AI can help leaders manage large-scale data, but it cannot inspire employees with genuine passion and empathy.

The future will belong to humans who use AI as an assistant, not a replacement, leveraging its analytical power while preserving the uniquely human traits of empathy, intuition, and emotional intelligence.

Despite AI's remarkable advancements, it remains incapable of replicating true human emotions, empathy, and moral reasoning. Emotional Intelligence is a uniquely human trait that defines how we connect, lead, and make ethical decisions.

While AI can assist in recognizing patterns and automating tasks, the ability to feel, relate, and care is something only humans can do.

As we integrate AI into our daily lives, we must ensure that technology serves as a partner rather than a replacement, allowing human emotional intelligence to remain at the core of meaningful interactions.

In the end, it is our emotions that make us truly human—and that is something no machine can ever replace.

SECTION 3: AI in Creativity and the Arts

Chapter 11: Can AI Be Creative? The Answer Might Surprise You

Creativity has long been considered a uniquely human trait—the ability to imagine, invent, and express emotions through art, music, literature, and problem-solving. However, with the rise of artificial intelligence, machines are now composing music, generating paintings, writing poetry, and even designing products. This raises an intriguing question: **Can AI truly be creative, or is it merely mimicking human creativity?**

The answer is not as straightforward as one might think. While AI can generate **remarkable works of art and ideas**, it lacks the emotional depth, intuition, and lived experiences that shape human creativity. In this chapter, we explore how AI is transforming creative fields, where its strengths and limitations lie, and why human imagination remains irreplaceable.

What Is Creativity?

Creativity is often defined as **the ability to produce original and meaningful work**. It involves:

- **Divergent Thinking** – Generating multiple ideas from a single prompt.
- **Problem-Solving** – Finding innovative solutions to complex challenges.
- **Emotional Expression** – Conveying feelings, perspectives, and experiences.

- **Cultural and Personal Influence** – Drawing inspiration from history, society, and personal experiences.

AI can process vast amounts of data and recognize patterns, but does this equate to **true creativity**?

How AI Is Being Used in Creative Fields

1. AI in Art and Design

AI-driven tools like DALL·E and DeepDream can generate stunning paintings, sketches, and digital art by analyzing thousands of existing works. Artists now use AI to **co-create** artwork, blending machine-generated elements with human intuition.

Example:

- AI-generated art has been auctioned for **hundreds of thousands of dollars**, like the painting **"Portrait of Edmond de Belamy,"** which sold for $432,500.

While AI can create aesthetically pleasing images, it lacks the personal **vision, intent, and storytelling** behind a masterpiece.

2. AI in Music Composition

AI-powered software like AIVA and OpenAI's MuseNet can **compose symphonies, jazz pieces, and pop songs** by studying vast libraries of musical compositions.

Example:

- AI has composed original **film scores and background music** for video games and advertisements.

However, while AI can generate harmonious compositions, it does not **feel emotion** or draw from personal experiences—something that gives human music its deep resonance.

3. AI in Writing and Storytelling

AI-generated writing tools like ChatGPT and Sudowrite can produce **stories, poetry, and scripts** based on prompts. AI even assists authors in brainstorming ideas and drafting content.

Example:

- An AI-written short story was shortlisted for a **literary competition**, showing that machines can produce **engaging narratives**.

Yet, while AI can construct well-formed sentences, it **lacks original thought, life experiences, and deep emotional nuance**—elements that make great literature stand out.

4. AI in Film and Media

AI is revolutionizing **scriptwriting, video editing, and CGI animation**. Filmmakers use AI to analyze audience preferences, optimize storytelling structures, and even create digital actors.

Example:

- AI-generated deepfake technology has been used to **recreate deceased actors** and modify scenes in movies.

Despite these advancements, AI does not **experience human emotions or cultural nuances**, making human input essential for storytelling.

What AI Can and Cannot Do in Creativity

☑ **What AI Can Do:**

- Analyze massive datasets to detect **patterns and trends**.

- Generate new **art, music, and stories** by recombining existing ideas.
- Assist in **idea generation** and **creative brainstorming**.
- Enhance human creativity by providing **suggestions and inspiration**.

❌ **What AI Cannot Do:**

- Experience **emotions, personal struggles, or human passion**.
- Create **art with deep intent, symbolism, and originality**.
- Make **intuitive leaps** that define groundbreaking creativity.
- Understand **cultural, historical, and emotional contexts** the way humans do.

Why Human Creativity Remains Unique

Despite AI's ability to generate artistic and literary content, **human creativity remains irreplaceable** for several reasons:

1. **Personal Experience Fuels Creativity**

Great works of art, literature, and music often stem from **personal struggles, emotions, and experiences**—something AI lacks.

- Van Gogh's **"Starry Night"** was inspired by his emotional turmoil.
- Beethoven's **Symphony No. 9** was composed despite his deafness.
- J.K. Rowling's **Harry Potter** was influenced by her personal hardships.

AI cannot **live, feel, or suffer**, making its creativity fundamentally **detached from human experience**.

2. **Creativity Requires Intuition and Risk-Taking**
   Human artists take **risks**, experiment with new styles, and break conventions—leading to revolutionary ideas. AI, however, **relies on past data** and struggles with unpredictability.

Example:

- Picasso's **Cubism** was a radical departure from traditional art—something AI would not invent on its own.

3. **Originality Comes from Human Vision**
   AI recombines existing knowledge, but **true innovation** comes from **human imagination**. Groundbreaking ideas often emerge **without precedent**—something AI, which depends on existing data, cannot achieve.

Example:

- The **Wright brothers** invented the airplane by dreaming of human flight, not by analyzing past failures alone.
4. **Creativity Is Deeply Emotional**
   Humans create art to **express joy, grief, love, and rebellion**. AI may generate a **heartfelt poem**, but it does not truly **understand pain, loss, or inspiration**.

Example:

- A machine can **mimic** Shakespearean sonnets but does not feel **heartache or longing**.

The Future: AI as a Creative Partner, not a Replacement

Rather than replacing human creativity, AI is best viewed as a **powerful tool that enhances human expression**. The future of creativity will likely involve **collaborations between AI and human artists**, where AI assists in idea generation, but humans provide **vision, meaning, and originality**.

AI + Human Creativity = Unprecedented Innovation

- AI can help musicians **experiment with new sounds**.
- AI can assist writers by **suggesting plot twists**.

- AI can generate **digital art**, but humans add the **soul and message.**

As AI continues to evolve, it will become a **co-creator**, allowing humans to push the boundaries of imagination while ensuring that creativity remains **deeply personal and uniquely human**.

AI can generate remarkable works of art, music, and literature, but **true creativity is more than just pattern recognition and recombination**. It is about **emotion, intuition, risk-taking, and originality**—qualities that AI cannot fully replicate.

Rather than fearing AI's role in creativity, we should embrace it as a **collaborative tool** that amplifies human potential. **The most powerful creations will come not from AI alone, but from the synergy of human ingenuity and artificial intelligence.**

In the end, AI can **generate** creativity, but only humans can **truly create with passion, purpose, and meaning.**

Chapter 12: AI and Human Collaboration in Music and Art

The worlds of music and art have long been considered realms of human imagination, emotion, and expression. However, the rise of artificial intelligence has introduced a fascinating shift—machines are now composing symphonies, painting masterpieces, and even designing innovative visual art. Rather than replacing human creativity, AI is emerging as a **collaborative partner**, enhancing artistic expression in ways never before possible.

From AI-generated paintings selling for hundreds of thousands of dollars to AI-assisted music compositions used in Hollywood films, the fusion of AI and human creativity is reshaping the artistic landscape. But how exactly does this collaboration work? Where does AI excel, and where does human ingenuity remain irreplaceable?

In this chapter, we explore how AI is transforming music and art, the ways humans and machines are working together, and why the human touch remains essential in creative expression.

AI in Music: Composing with Machines

1. AI as a Musician: The Rise of AI-Composed Music

AI-driven tools like **AIVA, OpenAI's MuseNet, and Google's Magenta** can compose music in various genres by analyzing patterns from classical symphonies, jazz, rock, and pop. These AI systems generate compositions that sound incredibly human-like.

Example:

- **AIVA (Artificial Intelligence Virtual Artist)** is recognized as an official composer and has created original symphonies that sound as if they were written by Mozart or Beethoven.

While AI can mimic musical styles, it does not **feel emotions, innovate intuitively, or understand cultural significance** the way human musicians do.

2. AI and Human Collaboration in Music Production

Instead of replacing composers, AI is being used as a tool to **enhance creativity** and **speed up music production**. Musicians use AI to:

- Generate **melody ideas** based on mood and style.
- Assist with **songwriting** by suggesting chords and harmonies.
- Provide **real-time mixing and mastering** for enhanced sound quality.

Example:

- AI-assisted music has been used in **film scores, advertisements, and video game soundtracks**, making production more efficient.

3. AI-Generated Songs vs. Human Creativity

AI can create original songs, but there are **clear limitations**:

✅ **What AI Can Do:**

- Generate new compositions based on existing musical styles.
- Suggest harmonies, chord progressions, and rhythm patterns.
- Improve sound engineering and audio production.

❌ **What AI Cannot Do:**

- **Feel emotions or personal experiences** that inspire music.
- Create songs with **deep lyrical meaning and storytelling**.
- Develop new **musical movements and genres** from intuition alone.

Human composers bring **raw emotion, cultural influence, and life experiences**, making their work deeply personal and unique. AI remains a **tool for inspiration, not a replacement for human artistry**.

AI in Visual Arts: A New Era of Creativity

1. AI-Generated Art: Machines as Digital Painters

AI art generators like **DALL·E, DeepDream, and Runway ML** can create stunning paintings, digital illustrations, and surreal images in seconds. These models analyze thousands of artworks to generate new visuals based on user prompts.

Example:

- AI-generated artwork **"Portrait of Edmond de Belamy"** was sold for **$432,500**, marking a milestone in AI's role in fine art.

However, while AI can produce visually impressive pieces, it **does not create with intention, passion, or life experiences**.

2. AI and Human Collaboration in Art

Artists are increasingly using AI as a creative partner rather than a competitor. AI helps with:

- **Generating initial concepts** for paintings, sculptures, and digital art.
- **Enhancing creativity** by providing unique style recommendations.
- **Automating tedious tasks**, such as image refinement and digital editing.

Example:

- Renowned artists like **Mario Klingemann** and **Refik Anadol** use AI to push the boundaries of digital art while maintaining human storytelling and vision.

3. Can AI Be a True Artist?

Despite AI's impressive capabilities, true artistry involves **emotion, cultural depth, and personal interpretation**.

✅ What AI Can Do:

- Analyze past artworks to create new visual styles.
- Generate realistic or abstract paintings with a given theme.
- Assist artists in expanding their creative ideas.

✖ What AI Cannot Do:

- Experience the **emotional struggles** that fuel artistic expression.
- Create art with **deep personal or societal meaning**.
- Innovate **new artistic movements** without human input.

Human artists infuse their work with **soul, intention, and lived experiences**—something AI-generated art lacks.

The Future of AI and Human Collaboration in Creativity

Rather than replacing artists and musicians, AI is becoming a **collaborative partner** that enhances human creativity. The **future of AI in art and music lies in synergy, not competition**.

Key trends shaping the future:

1. **AI-Assisted Creativity:** Artists and musicians will increasingly use AI as a **co-creator** to generate ideas and experiment with styles.
2. **Human Emotion + AI Efficiency:** While AI can assist with technical aspects, human emotion will always be the **soul of creative works**.

3. **New Art Forms and Music Genres:** The fusion of AI and human creativity may lead to **entirely new artistic movements and music genres.**

AI + Human Creativity = Unprecedented Innovation

- AI **enhances** human creativity but does not **replace it.**
- The best music and art will come from a **collaboration between human imagination and AI's computational power.**
- **Artists and musicians will always be at the center** of creative expression, with AI acting as a tool to push boundaries.

AI has transformed the creative landscape in music and art, but **it remains a tool rather than a true creator.** While AI can compose melodies, paint masterpieces, and generate digital art, **it lacks the emotional depth, personal vision, and cultural nuance that define true artistry.**

Rather than fearing AI's role in creativity, artists and musicians should embrace it as a **collaborative partner** that **enhances inspiration, expands possibilities, and accelerates creative processes.**

In the end, **human creativity is not being replaced—it is being amplified.** The greatest artistic achievements will come not from AI alone, but from **the fusion of human passion and machine intelligence**.

Chapter 13: The Future of AI in Literature and Storytelling

*Storytelling has been at the heart of human civilization for thousands of years. From ancient myths and folklore to modern novels and screenplays, stories shape how we understand the world and express emotions, ideas, and culture. With the rise of artificial intelligence, the landscape of literature and storytelling is undergoing a transformation. AI is now capable of **generating poetry, writing short stories, and even assisting in novel writing**, raising profound questions:*

- Can AI truly create compelling narratives?
- Will AI replace human authors, or will it serve as a creative assistant?
- How will AI reshape the publishing industry and storytelling techniques?

This chapter explores **AI's role in literature and storytelling**, how it complements human creativity, and what the future holds for AI-assisted storytelling.

AI in Literature: A New Age of Writing

1. AI as an Author: Can Machines Write?

AI-powered language models like **ChatGPT, GPT-4, and Bard** can now generate complex narratives, poetry, and even entire books. These systems analyze vast amounts of literature and predict the most coherent and engaging ways to structure stories.

Examples:

- **AI-generated novels** have already been submitted for literary awards.
- AI has been used to **continue unfinished works** by famous authors.
- **Poetry and short stories** written by AI have been published and admired for their artistic quality.

However, while AI can produce well-structured narratives, it lacks the **deep emotions, personal experiences, and philosophical insights** that make literature uniquely human.

2. AI as a Writing Assistant: Enhancing Human Creativity

Instead of replacing authors, AI is proving to be a **powerful tool for writers**. Many novelists and scriptwriters now use AI for:

- **Idea generation:** AI suggests themes, character arcs, and plotlines.
- **Overcoming writer's block:** AI provides prompts and alternative story developments.
- **Editing and style refinement:** AI helps improve grammar, coherence, and pacing.
- **Generating dialogue:** AI assists in crafting realistic conversations.

Example:

- Screenwriters and novelists use AI to **experiment with different story endings** and improve dialogue before finalizing their manuscripts.

AI is becoming an **essential partner in creative writing**, but the core storytelling **remains human-driven**.

The Role of AI in Storytelling

1. AI-Generated Stories vs. Human Creativity

AI can analyze existing works and generate new stories, but does that mean it can **replace human authors**?

☑ **What AI Can Do:**

- Write grammatically sound, structured narratives.
- Mimic different writing styles and genres.
- Suggest creative ideas and alternative storylines.
- Help streamline the editing and publishing process.

✕ What AI Cannot Do:

- **Experience human emotions** or translate personal struggles into stories.
- Create narratives with **deep philosophical meaning**.
- Develop **original storytelling styles** beyond what it has been trained on.
- Capture **cultural and historical nuances** without human guidance.

Human authors bring **lived experiences, emotional intelligence, and artistic depth** to literature—qualities AI cannot replicate.

2. AI in Screenwriting and Film Storytelling

Hollywood and the entertainment industry are already experimenting with AI-generated scripts. AI can:

- **Develop screenplay structures** based on hit movies.
- **Generate realistic dialogues** for characters.

- **Assist in script revisions and scene development.**

However, the most compelling movies and TV shows come from **human creativity, emotions, and cultural storytelling traditions**. AI can assist, but **directors, screenwriters, and actors will always be at the core of storytelling.**

AI and the Future of Publishing

1. AI's Impact on Self-Publishing and Content Creation

With AI-driven writing tools, **self-publishing is becoming more accessible.** Authors can use AI to:

- Generate **outlines and drafts** quickly.
- Optimize their manuscripts for **readability and engagement**.
- Translate their books into **multiple languages** using AI-powered translation tools.
- Automate **audiobook narration** with AI-generated voices.

AI-powered publishing tools will **reduce costs and improve efficiency,** making it easier for aspiring writers to get their work into the world.

2. AI and Personalized Storytelling

AI is paving the way for **interactive and personalized storytelling**, where readers can shape the story's outcome. Future AI-powered books may allow:

- **Choose-your-own-adventure storytelling**, where AI adjusts the plot based on reader preferences.
- **AI-generated narratives tailored to individual tastes**, such as specific genres, characters, or themes.
- **Virtual reality (VR) storytelling**, where AI creates immersive, real-time story experiences.

The future of literature may involve **dynamic, AI-assisted storytelling**, but human authors will remain at the heart of crafting compelling narratives.

The Human-AI Partnership in Literature

AI will not replace human authors—it will **empower them**. The best storytelling will come from a **collaboration between AI's computational abilities and human emotional depth**.

Key trends shaping the future of AI in literature:

1. **AI-assisted creativity:** Writers will use AI for idea generation, editing, and plot structuring.
2. **Interactive storytelling:** AI will enable new forms of personalized and immersive narratives.
3. **AI-enhanced publishing:** Automation will streamline the self-publishing process.
4. **Human-driven storytelling remains supreme:** While AI can assist, true literary artistry will always require the human touch.

AI is revolutionizing literature and storytelling, but it is not replacing the **human art of storytelling**. Instead, it is providing authors, poets, and screenwriters with **new tools to enhance creativity, refine writing, and explore new narrative possibilities**.

While AI can generate structured and engaging stories, the **soul of literature—the emotions, struggles, experiences, and artistic depth—remains uniquely human**. The future of storytelling lies not in AI alone, but in the **powerful synergy between human imagination and machine intelligence**.

Chapter 14: AI in Film, Animation, and Gaming

The entertainment industry has always been at the forefront of technological evolution. From the early days of hand-drawn animation to CGI-driven blockbusters, technology has continuously reshaped storytelling. Today, **artificial intelligence (AI) is revolutionizing film, animation, and gaming**, enhancing creativity, efficiency, and audience engagement.

AI is now playing a crucial role in:

- **Scriptwriting and content generation**
- **Visual effects (VFX) and animation automation**
- **Voice synthesis and deepfake technology**
- **Game development and intelligent NPCs (non-player characters)**
- **Personalized storytelling and adaptive gaming**

As AI becomes more advanced, it is **reshaping how movies are made, animations are created, and games are played**. But does this mean AI will replace human creativity? This chapter explores how AI is transforming these industries while working alongside human artists and creators.

AI in the Film Industry

1. AI in Scriptwriting and Pre-Production

AI is increasingly being used to assist in scriptwriting, analyzing successful story patterns, and generating dialogues. Some AI-powered tools can:

- **Analyze past hit movies** and suggest story structures.
- **Generate dialogues** based on character profiles.
- **Suggest scene sequences** based on audience preferences.

Examples:

- **ScriptBook** uses AI to analyze screenplays and predict their commercial success.
- AI-generated short films, such as "Sunspring," have demonstrated how AI can create experimental scripts.

However, while AI can help with plot structuring, **human writers bring emotional depth, cultural nuance, and originality** that AI cannot replicate.

2. AI in Visual Effects (VFX) and CGI

AI is revolutionizing **visual effects and CGI (computer-generated imagery),** making processes faster and more efficient. AI-driven tools can:

- **Create realistic facial animations** without extensive motion capture.
- **De-age actors or digitally resurrect them**, as seen in Star Wars films.
- **Automatically remove green screens** and enhance backgrounds.

Examples:

- **Deepfake technology** was used to bring back young versions of actors in *The Irishman*.
- AI-generated landscapes and creatures reduce the need for expensive CGI teams.

While AI speeds up VFX work, **human artists and designers remain essential for creativity and storytelling impact**.

3. AI and Voice Synthesis in Film

AI-generated voices are now being used to:

- **Dub movies into multiple languages** with realistic lip-syncing.

- **Recreate the voices of deceased actors** (e.g., James Earl Jones' AI-generated Darth Vader voice).
- **Generate narration for documentaries and animated films.**

Although AI voice synthesis is impressive, **human voice actors bring emotion and authenticity** that AI has yet to fully replicate.

AI in Animation

1. AI-Powered Animation Tools

Animation is traditionally time-consuming, but AI is changing the process with:

- **Automated motion capture** using AI-based body tracking.
- **Style transfer AI** to mimic different animation styles.
- **AI-generated in-between frames** to smooth character movements.

Examples:

- **Disney uses AI to enhance animation workflows.**

- **Runway ML and DeepMotion** allow animators to create realistic movements with minimal effort.

While AI enhances efficiency, the artistic vision of animators remains **the heart of storytelling** in animation.

2. AI in Character Animation and Lip Syncing

AI-powered tools now allow characters to:

- **Automatically generate realistic lip movements** for any language.
- **Mimic human facial expressions and emotions**.
- **Adapt to real-time motion capture data.**

Example:

- **Adobe's AI-driven Character Animator** helps animators bring characters to life in real-time.

Despite these advancements, animators still play a crucial role in **character personality, style, and emotional expression**.

AI in Gaming

1. AI in Game Development

AI is revolutionizing how video games are created, making game development **faster and more efficient**. AI tools help with:

- **Procedural content generation**, creating game levels automatically.
- **AI-driven storylines** that adapt based on player choices.
- **Character behavior modeling**, making NPCs more intelligent.

Examples:

- **No Man's Sky** uses AI-generated planets and creatures.
- **AI Dungeon** creates text-based adventure stories using AI-generated narratives.

While AI speeds up development, game designers and writers **still define the heart of a game's story and experience**.

2. AI in Non-Player Character (NPC) Behavior

AI is making **NPCs smarter and more interactive**, enhancing the gaming experience. NPCs can now:

- **Adapt to player behavior and learn over time.**
- **Engage in realistic conversations with AI-driven dialogues.**
- **Exhibit unique personalities and decision-making abilities.**

Example:

- **Red Dead Redemption 2** features AI-driven NPCs that react dynamically to the player's actions.

While AI makes NPCs more realistic, human developers still design **narrative depth and engaging interactions**.

3. AI in Personalized Gaming Experiences

AI-driven algorithms **personalize gaming** by:

- Adjusting difficulty levels based on player skill.
- Creating custom quests and challenges in open-world games.
- Tailoring in-game music and environments to match player mood.

Example:

- **AI in The Sims adapts characters' personalities** based on player interactions.

As AI continues to evolve, gaming will become **more immersive and responsive**, but human creativity remains essential for compelling storytelling.

The Future of AI in Film, Animation, and Gaming

1. AI as a Creative Partner, not a Replacement

AI is transforming film, animation, and gaming, but it is not replacing human creators. Instead, it:

- ☑ Enhances creativity by automating repetitive tasks.

- ☑ Improves efficiency in animation and visual effects.

- ☑ Enables more personalized and interactive storytelling.

However, AI **lacks emotional depth, artistic intuition, and cultural storytelling expertise**, which remain uniquely human.

2. Ethical Concerns and Challenges

As AI becomes more prevalent, it raises concerns:

- **AI-generated actors and ethical boundaries** (e.g., using deepfake technology).
- **Job displacement in the entertainment industry.**
- **Over-reliance on AI-generated content, reducing originality.**

To balance AI's benefits and challenges, **human oversight and ethical guidelines are necessary.**

3. The Future: Human-AI Collaboration

The future of AI in entertainment lies in **collaboration between humans and AI:**

- Writers will **use AI as a brainstorming assistant.**
- Animators will **leverage AI for faster rendering and motion capture.**
- Game developers will **create richer, AI-driven interactive worlds.**

Rather than replacing human artists, **AI will serve as a tool to unlock new creative possibilities.**

AI is revolutionizing **film, animation, and gaming,** making them more immersive, interactive, and efficient. While AI can generate content, automate animation, and enhance game design, **human creativity remains the driving force** behind compelling storytelling.

The future of entertainment will be shaped by **a dynamic partnership between AI and human creators**, leading to **more engaging, personalized, and boundary-pushing experiences**.

Chapter 15: Human Creativity vs. AI-Generated Art

Art has always been a profound expression of human emotions, culture, and imagination. From the cave paintings of early humans to the masterpieces of Da Vinci and Van Gogh, creativity has been an inherently human trait. However, with the rise of artificial intelligence, a new era has emerged where machines can generate art, compose music, and even write poetry. This raises important questions. Can AI-generated art truly compare to human creativity? Does AI create, or does it simply replicate patterns it has learned? Is AI an artist, a tool, or a mere imitator? This chapter explores the differences, strengths, and limitations of human creativity versus AI-generated art.

The Rise of AI-Generated Art

AI-generated art is powered by machine learning algorithms, particularly deep learning models. Generative Adversarial Networks (GANs) are used to create realistic images, paintings, and deepfake videos.

Neural Style Transfer (NST) allows AI to apply artistic styles to images, making a photograph resemble a Van Gogh painting. Natural Language Processing (NLP) models assist in AI-generated poetry, storytelling, and lyrics.

The field of AI-generated art has grown significantly. Tools like DALL·E and Midjourney create paintings based on text descriptions, while AIVA, an Artificial Intelligence Virtual Artist, composes classical music. Google's DeepDream produces surreal, dreamlike images. AI is also revolutionizing digital art and design by generating new visual styles, automating background and character creation, and assisting graphic designers and illustrators in concept development.

One of the most striking examples of AI-generated art was the portrait *Portrait of Edmond de Belamy*, which was auctioned for $432,500 at Christie's in 2018. The sale of this artwork demonstrated that AI-generated creations can hold significant value. However, does AI truly create, or does it simply recombine existing data?

What Makes Human Creativity Unique?

Human creativity is deeply personal. Art reflects emotions, experiences, and cultural influences in ways that AI cannot replicate. Every brushstroke, lyric, or verse carries intent and meaning shaped by the artist's unique perspective. Unlike AI, which relies on data and learned patterns, human creativity is often driven by emotions and subjective experiences. Artists express their struggles, dreams, and emotions in ways that AI cannot because machines do not feel. Cultural and historical context also play a crucial role in shaping artistic expression, something AI lacks. Human artists innovate and break rules intentionally, whereas AI simply follows patterns it has learned.

Storytelling and symbolism further distinguish human creativity from AI-generated work. Human artists infuse their creations with deeper narratives, metaphors, and symbolism, elements that AI struggles to comprehend. Leonardo da Vinci's *Mona Lisa* is famous not just for its technique but for the mystery behind the subject's expression. AI can generate a face, a painting, or a melody, but can it weave a story that resonates with human experiences?

AI vs. Human Art: Strengths and Weaknesses

While AI can generate artwork quickly and with technical precision, it lacks originality, emotion, and deeper meaning. Human creativity involves true innovation and unique perspectives, whereas AI learns from existing data and recombines styles. AI-generated art can be visually stunning, but it often lacks the emotional depth and personal meaning that human artists bring to their work. Context and symbolism play a significant role in human art, while AI struggles to understand cultural and historical significance.

Creativity also requires adaptability and the ability to break norms. Artists such as Picasso, who pioneered the Cubist movement, challenged traditional artistic rules in ways that AI would not have independently developed. On the other hand, AI excels in speed and efficiency. It can generate hundreds of artworks in seconds, making it a useful tool for artists seeking inspiration or assistance in the creative process.

Is AI an Artist or a Tool?

AI should not be seen as a competitor to human creativity but as a collaborative partner. Many artists use AI as a tool to enhance their work rather than replace their own creativity. AI assists in brainstorming concepts, composing melodies, and automating repetitive tasks in animation and game design. Musician Taryn Southern, for example, used AI to compose an entire album, blending human creativity with AI-generated melodies.

The rise of AI-generated art also raises ethical questions. Ownership of AI-created art remains a contentious issue. Does the programmer, the AI, or the person who provided the input prompt own the final piece? The debate over whether AI-generated art "steals" from human artists also continues. AI is trained on vast datasets of human-created works, leading to concerns about copyright infringement. Additionally, some fear that AI will replace artists altogether. However, while AI can generate art, human artists still bring depth, emotion, and originality that machines cannot replicate.

The Future of AI and Human Creativity

Rather than viewing AI as a competitor, artists can use it as a creative amplifier. The future of AI and human creativity lies in collaboration rather than replacement. AI can serve as a tool to enhance artistic expression, allowing humans to push the boundaries of creativity while maintaining the emotional and symbolic depth that makes art meaningful. The debate over AI and creativity will continue, but one thing remains clear: human ingenuity, emotion, and innovation will always play a central role in artistic expression.

SECTION 4: AI in Business and Innovation

Chapter 16: AI as a Business Partner: Enhancing Human Productivity

Artificial intelligence has transitioned from a futuristic concept to a fundamental part of the modern business world. While many fear AI may replace jobs and reduce human involvement, the reality is quite the opposite. AI is proving to be an invaluable business partner, enhancing human productivity, streamlining operations, and enabling professionals to focus on strategic and creative tasks. Whether through automating repetitive processes, optimizing decision-making, or providing insights from vast data pools, AI is transforming industries and helping businesses achieve unprecedented efficiency.

AI's Role in Business Efficiency

One of the most significant advantages of AI in the workplace is its ability to automate routine tasks. AI-powered tools handle data entry, financial reporting, scheduling, and customer service inquiries, freeing up employees to focus on higher-value work. In industries such as manufacturing, AI-driven robotics and automation optimize production lines, reduce waste, and improve safety.

AI also enhances productivity by acting as a decision-making assistant. Predictive analytics tools analyze historical and real-time data to identify patterns, helping businesses make informed decisions. For instance, AI can forecast market trends, assess risks, and recommend strategies for growth. Companies use AI-powered chatbots and virtual assistants to handle customer inquiries, reducing response times and improving customer satisfaction.

AI in Human Resource Management

AI is transforming human resource management by optimizing recruitment, training, and employee engagement. AI-powered applicant tracking systems scan resumes and identify the most qualified candidates, significantly reducing the time spent on hiring. Some companies use AI chatbots to conduct initial interviews, assessing a candidate's responses before a human interviewer steps in.

AI also helps in performance evaluation and employee development. Machine learning algorithms analyze work patterns, providing feedback on employee performance and suggesting personalized training programs. This approach ensures employees continue to develop their skills while improving overall workplace efficiency.

AI in Marketing and Customer Engagement

Marketing has been revolutionized by AI, making it more data-driven and personalized. AI-powered analytics tools track customer behavior, preferences, and purchasing history, allowing businesses to create targeted marketing campaigns. Personalized recommendations, such as those used by Amazon and Netflix, improve customer engagement and increase sales.

Social media management also benefits from AI-driven automation. AI tools schedule posts, analyze audience interactions, and optimize content strategies. Chatbots and virtual assistants engage customers in real-time, answering queries, resolving issues, and providing personalized recommendations.

AI in Finance and Business Decision-Making

In the financial sector, AI is helping businesses manage investments, detect fraud, and optimize financial planning. AI-driven trading algorithms analyze vast amounts of market data to identify profitable investment opportunities. Fraud detection systems use AI to monitor transactions for unusual patterns, alerting financial institutions to potential security threats.

Businesses also leverage AI for budgeting and forecasting. AI analyzes historical financial data and market trends to predict future expenses and revenue. This allows businesses to make more informed financial decisions and allocate resources efficiently.

AI in Supply Chain and Logistics

AI has transformed supply chain management by improving efficiency and reducing costs. Predictive analytics help businesses anticipate demand fluctuations, ensuring optimal inventory levels and minimizing waste. AI-driven logistics solutions optimize delivery routes, reducing fuel costs and improving delivery times.

Warehouse automation, powered by AI and robotics, streamlines inventory management. Automated systems track stock levels, manage order fulfillment, and reduce errors. Companies like Amazon use AI-driven robots to enhance warehouse operations, significantly increasing productivity.

The Human-AI Collaboration in Business

While AI enhances efficiency, human intuition, creativity, and ethical judgment remain irreplaceable. AI can process vast amounts of data and identify patterns, but humans provide strategic vision, emotional intelligence, and ethical considerations. The ideal business model involves collaboration between AI and humans, where AI handles data-driven tasks, and humans focus on innovation and decision-making.

For example, AI can analyze consumer trends, but marketing professionals interpret the data creatively to design compelling campaigns. AI can suggest financial investments, but human advisors consider ethical and long-term implications before making final decisions.

Challenges and Ethical Considerations

Despite its benefits, AI in business comes with challenges. Data privacy concerns arise as AI systems collect and analyze vast amounts of personal information. Businesses must implement strict security measures to protect customer data and comply with regulations.

Another concern is the potential for job displacement. While AI automates tasks, it also creates new job opportunities, particularly in AI development, maintenance, and human-AI collaboration roles. Companies must invest in upskilling employees to prepare them for an AI-driven future.

The Future of AI in Business

The future of AI in business is promising, with advancements in machine learning, natural language processing, and automation driving innovation. Businesses that embrace AI as a partner rather than a replacement will gain a competitive advantage. AI will continue to enhance productivity, optimize operations, and support human decision-making, ultimately leading to more efficient and innovative workplaces.

As AI evolves, businesses must strike a balance between automation and human expertise. By leveraging AI's analytical capabilities while valuing human creativity and ethical judgment, companies can maximize productivity and create a more dynamic and successful future.

Chapter 17: AI in Entrepreneurship and Startups

Artificial intelligence is revolutionizing the startup ecosystem, enabling entrepreneurs to innovate, scale, and compete in ways that were once unimaginable. AI-driven tools and solutions provide startups with the ability to automate processes, analyze vast amounts of data, enhance customer experiences, and optimize decision-making. Unlike large corporations with abundant resources, startups often operate with limited capital and manpower. AI levels the playing field by offering cost-effective solutions that enhance efficiency, creativity, and strategic growth.

AI as a Startup Accelerator

For entrepreneurs, AI acts as an accelerator, streamlining various business functions from product development to customer engagement. AI-powered chatbots handle customer inquiries, reducing the need for large customer service teams. Predictive analytics tools analyze market trends, helping startups make data-driven decisions. AI-driven marketing tools personalize advertising campaigns, increasing engagement and conversion rates. These capabilities allow startups to scale rapidly with minimal overhead costs.

AI in Market Research and Competitive Analysis

One of the biggest challenges for startups is identifying market opportunities and understanding competition. AI-powered tools analyze consumer behavior, industry trends, and competitor strategies, providing startups with valuable insights. Machine learning algorithms process large datasets to identify emerging trends, allowing entrepreneurs to refine their business models and stay ahead of competitors.

Startups can also leverage AI for sentiment analysis, examining customer reviews and social media interactions to gauge public perception of their brand. This real-time feedback helps entrepreneurs adjust their marketing strategies and improve their products or services based on customer needs.

AI-Driven Product Development and Innovation

AI plays a crucial role in product development by enabling startups to design, prototype, and refine products efficiently. AI-powered design tools generate innovative product concepts based on market demand and user preferences. For example, AI-assisted software can create multiple design variations for a new product, allowing entrepreneurs to select the most viable option.

Startups in sectors such as healthcare, fintech, and e-commerce use AI to develop smart products and services. AI-driven diagnostic tools assist in early disease detection, AI-powered financial advisors provide personalized investment guidance, and AI-enabled recommendation engines enhance online shopping experiences. These innovations not only improve customer satisfaction but also drive business growth.

AI in Automating Business Operations

Entrepreneurs often juggle multiple responsibilities, from managing finances to overseeing marketing campaigns. AI automates routine tasks, freeing up time for entrepreneurs to focus on strategic decision-making. AI-powered accounting software manages invoices, expenses, and financial reports with precision. AI-driven HR tools streamline recruitment, employee onboarding, and performance management.

Supply chain and logistics automation also benefit startups by optimizing inventory management and delivery processes. AI predicts demand fluctuations, ensuring optimal stock levels and reducing waste.

Logistics startups use AI-powered route optimization to minimize delivery costs and improve efficiency.

AI-Powered Marketing and Customer Engagement

Marketing is a vital aspect of startup success, and AI is transforming the way businesses engage with customers. AI-driven digital marketing platforms analyze user behavior, optimizing ad placements for maximum impact. Personalized content recommendations enhance customer engagement and loyalty.

Chatbots and virtual assistants handle customer inquiries, providing instant responses and improving user experience. AI-powered email marketing tools segment audiences based on preferences, sending targeted messages that boost conversion rates. Startups leveraging AI in their marketing strategies gain a competitive edge by delivering hyper-personalized customer experiences.

AI in Fundraising and Investment Decisions

Securing funding is a major challenge for startups, and AI is making the process more efficient. AI-driven investment platforms analyze financial data and business models to assess a startup's growth potential. Entrepreneurs use AI to create compelling pitch decks, highlighting key metrics and market opportunities.

Venture capital firms and investors leverage AI to evaluate startups, assessing risk factors and predicting long-term success. AI-powered financial modeling tools simulate different growth scenarios, helping startups present data-driven projections to potential investors.

Challenges and Ethical Considerations

While AI offers numerous benefits to entrepreneurs, it also presents challenges. Startups must navigate issues related to data privacy, algorithm bias, and ethical AI use. Relying too heavily on AI without human oversight can lead to flawed decision-making. Entrepreneurs must ensure that AI-driven insights align with ethical business practices.

Another challenge is the initial cost of AI implementation. Although AI-driven tools can enhance efficiency, acquiring and integrating AI technology may require significant investment. Startups must weigh the benefits of AI adoption against budget constraints and prioritize AI solutions that deliver the highest return on investment.

The Future of AI in Startups

As AI continues to evolve, its role in entrepreneurship will expand. AI-powered no-code and low-code development platforms enable startups to build applications without extensive programming knowledge. AI-driven virtual assistants will provide entrepreneurs with real-time business insights, enhancing strategic planning.

The future of AI in startups lies in human-AI collaboration. AI will handle data-intensive tasks, while entrepreneurs focus on creativity, leadership, and innovation. Startups that embrace AI as a strategic partner will be better positioned for growth, disruption, and long-term success in the competitive business landscape.

By integrating AI-driven solutions thoughtfully and ethically, entrepreneurs can unlock new opportunities, optimize efficiency, and build scalable, sustainable businesses in the digital age.

Chapter 18: The Role of AI in Market Analysis and Predictions

Market analysis and forecasting have always been crucial for businesses seeking to understand consumer behavior, industry trends, and future market conditions. With the rapid advancements in artificial intelligence, companies can now leverage AI-powered tools to analyze vast datasets, predict trends, and make data-driven decisions with remarkable accuracy. AI-driven market analysis is transforming industries by providing real-time insights, automating research, and improving the precision of business strategies.

How AI is Transforming Market Analysis

Traditional market analysis relied on manual research, surveys, and historical data. While these methods provided valuable insights, they were often time-consuming, prone to human error, and limited in scope. AI revolutionizes market analysis by processing large volumes of data quickly and efficiently.

Machine learning algorithms analyze consumer behavior, social media trends, and economic indicators to identify patterns that might not be apparent through traditional methods. AI-powered tools continuously monitor global events, news, and financial markets to provide businesses with up-to-date insights, allowing them to adapt their strategies in real time.

Predicting Consumer Behavior with AI

AI helps businesses understand their customers by analyzing past interactions, purchasing habits, and preferences. Predictive analytics use machine learning to anticipate customer needs, enabling companies to tailor their marketing strategies accordingly.

For instance, e-commerce platforms use AI-driven recommendation engines to suggest products based on a user's browsing history. Streaming services like Netflix and Spotify analyze user preferences to recommend movies, TV shows, and music. These AI-driven insights enhance customer experiences, increasing engagement and sales.

Retailers also use AI to forecast demand for specific products. By analyzing sales patterns, seasonal trends, and external factors such as weather or economic conditions, AI helps businesses optimize inventory management and prevent stock shortages or overproduction.

AI in Financial Market Predictions

One of the most impactful applications of AI in market analysis is in the financial sector. AI-powered trading algorithms analyze stock market data, news sentiment, and macroeconomic indicators to predict stock price movements. These algorithms execute trades at lightning speed, providing investors with a competitive edge.

Hedge funds and investment firms leverage AI to identify profitable investment opportunities and manage risk. AI-powered robo-advisors assist retail investors by providing personalized portfolio recommendations based on risk tolerance and financial goals. By eliminating human bias and emotions, AI enhances the accuracy of financial market predictions.

Sentiment Analysis and Social Media Monitoring

AI-driven sentiment analysis helps businesses gauge public opinion on brands, products, and industry trends. Natural language processing (NLP) algorithms analyze customer reviews, social media comments, and online discussions to assess consumer sentiment.

For example, if a new product launch receives negative feedback on social media, AI can detect the sentiment shift and alert businesses to take corrective action. Companies can also use AI-powered tools to monitor competitor strategies and customer feedback, gaining valuable insights to refine their marketing and branding efforts.

AI in Economic Forecasting

Governments, businesses, and financial institutions rely on economic forecasting to make informed decisions. AI enhances economic predictions by analyzing historical data, employment rates, inflation trends, and global trade patterns.

For instance, AI can predict economic recessions by identifying early warning signals in financial markets and global trade activities. AI-driven economic models help policymakers make data-driven decisions regarding interest rates, taxation, and monetary policies. Businesses use these insights to prepare for economic fluctuations and adjust their long-term strategies accordingly.

Personalized Marketing and Consumer Targeting

AI-driven marketing strategies have revolutionized how companies target their customers. By analyzing user behavior and preferences, AI creates personalized marketing campaigns tailored to specific audiences.

Email marketing automation tools use AI to send personalized messages based on a customer's interests and past purchases. AI-powered chatbots engage with customers in real time, providing product recommendations and answering queries. These AI-driven solutions enhance customer experiences while increasing conversion rates and brand loyalty.

Predictive marketing tools also help companies allocate their advertising budgets efficiently. AI analyzes which marketing channels generate the highest return on investment, allowing businesses to optimize their ad placements and maximize revenue.

Challenges and Ethical Considerations

Despite its benefits, AI-driven market analysis comes with challenges. One major concern is data privacy. AI systems require vast amounts of personal data to generate insights, raising ethical questions about consumer privacy and data security. Businesses must implement strict data protection measures to ensure compliance with privacy regulations.

Another challenge is algorithmic bias. AI models are trained on historical data, and if this data contains biases, the AI system may produce skewed predictions. For example, biased hiring algorithms can lead to discriminatory hiring practices. Companies must regularly audit their AI systems to ensure fairness and transparency.

Additionally, reliance on AI for decision-making should not eliminate human oversight. AI can provide accurate predictions, but human intuition and judgment remain essential for interpreting data in complex and unpredictable situations. Businesses should adopt a hybrid approach where AI augments human expertise rather than replacing it.

The Future of AI in Market Analysis

AI's role in market analysis and predictions will continue to expand as technology evolves. Future advancements in AI, such as quantum computing and advanced deep learning models, will further enhance predictive accuracy.

Businesses that embrace AI-driven market analysis will gain a competitive advantage by making data-driven decisions with greater speed and precision. AI will continue to shape industries by enabling hyper-personalized marketing, optimizing financial investments, and predicting consumer trends with unparalleled accuracy.

In the coming years, AI will not only transform how businesses analyze markets but also redefine how they interact with customers, develop products, and drive innovation. By leveraging AI responsibly and ethically, businesses can unlock new growth opportunities and navigate the ever-changing market landscape with confidence.

Chapter 19: AI-Powered Leadership and Decision-Making

In today's fast-paced world, effective leadership and decision-making are crucial for success in business, politics, healthcare, and other fields. The emergence of artificial intelligence has introduced a transformative shift, empowering leaders with data-driven insights, predictive analytics, and real-time decision-making support. AI is not here to replace human leaders but to enhance their capabilities, enabling them to make better, faster, and more informed decisions.

By integrating AI into leadership strategies, organizations can reduce uncertainty, improve operational efficiency, and navigate complex challenges with greater confidence. However, AI-powered decision-making also comes with ethical concerns and limitations, making it essential for leaders to strike the right balance between human judgment and machine intelligence.

How AI Enhances Leadership

Leadership has traditionally been associated with vision, experience, and intuition. While these qualities remain essential, AI introduces a new dimension by providing leaders with real-time insights, scenario analysis, and data-backed recommendations.

1. **Data-Driven Decision-Making**

2. AI processes massive datasets far beyond human capacity, identifying patterns, correlations, and anomalies that might go unnoticed. This allows leaders to base their decisions on comprehensive, objective data rather than gut instinct alone. For example, AI-

powered business intelligence platforms analyze financial trends, customer behavior, and market conditions to help executives formulate strategic plans.

3. Predictive Analytics for Risk Management

AI's predictive capabilities enable leaders to anticipate risks and take proactive measures. In finance, AI models detect potential economic downturns, fraudulent activities, or investment opportunities. In healthcare, AI predicts disease outbreaks and patient health risks, allowing medical leaders to allocate resources effectively. By leveraging AI-driven foresight, leaders can mitigate risks before they escalate into crises.

4. Enhanced Crisis Management

During emergencies, rapid and accurate decision-making is critical. AI-powered tools assist leaders in crisis management by analyzing real-time data, simulating various response scenarios, and recommending optimal courses of action. Governments use AI to predict and manage natural disasters, while businesses rely on AI-driven cybersecurity systems to detect and neutralize threats before they cause significant damage.

5. Optimizing Human Resource Management

AI is revolutionizing HR leadership by improving recruitment, employee engagement, and performance analysis. AI-powered algorithms assess job candidates based on skills, experience, and cultural fit, reducing hiring biases. Additionally, AI-driven employee sentiment analysis helps leaders understand workplace morale, allowing them to implement policies that enhance productivity and job satisfaction.

6. Automating Routine Decisions

AI allows leaders to focus on high-level strategic decisions by automating routine and operational choices. AI chatbots handle customer service inquiries, AI-powered supply chain systems optimize inventory management, and AI-driven financial software automates budgeting and forecasting. By delegating repetitive tasks to AI, leaders can concentrate on innovation, long-term planning, and creative problem-solving.

AI and Ethical Leadership

While AI provides numerous advantages, ethical considerations must be addressed to ensure responsible AI-powered leadership.

1. Transparency and Accountability

Leaders must ensure that AI-driven decisions are transparent and explainable. Black-box AI models, where decision-making processes are unclear, can erode trust and accountability. Organizations should implement explainable AI (XAI) systems that provide clear insights into how AI reaches its conclusions.

2. Avoiding Bias in AI

AI models learn from historical data, which may contain biases. If left unchecked, AI can reinforce discriminatory practices in hiring, lending, law enforcement, and other areas. Ethical leaders must actively audit AI systems to identify and mitigate biases, ensuring fairness and inclusivity.

3. Balancing AI with Human Judgment

AI should complement, not replace, human decision-making. Leaders must use AI insights as a guide rather than an absolute directive. Human intuition, creativity, and ethical reasoning remain irreplaceable, particularly in complex moral and social dilemmas.

AI in Government and Policy-Making

Governments worldwide are integrating AI into policy-making, urban planning, and national security. AI-driven data analysis helps policymakers assess economic trends, monitor public health, and design sustainable infrastructure projects.

For example, AI-powered traffic management systems optimize city transport networks, reducing congestion and pollution. AI also aids in national security by analyzing intelligence reports, detecting cyber threats, and improving law enforcement efficiency. However, government leaders must balance AI's benefits with privacy concerns, ensuring that AI applications align with democratic values and civil rights.

AI in Business Leadership

Business leaders are leveraging AI to optimize operations, improve customer experiences, and drive innovation. AI-powered market analysis tools help executives anticipate industry trends, identify growth opportunities, and refine marketing strategies. AI-driven automation streamlines production, reducing costs and increasing efficiency.

Tech giants like Google, Amazon, and Tesla use AI to enhance decision-making in product development, logistics, and customer service. Startups and small businesses also benefit from AI-driven analytics, allowing them to compete with larger corporations on a data-driven playing field.

The Future of AI-Powered Leadership

As AI technology advances, its role in leadership and decision-making will continue to expand. Future developments in AI-driven leadership may include:

- **AI-Powered Virtual Advisors**: Leaders may work alongside AI advisors that provide real-time insights, scenario simulations, and strategic recommendations.
- **Human-AI Collaboration Models**: Organizations may develop leadership structures where AI systems and human executives share decision-making responsibilities.
- **Emotionally Intelligent AI**: Future AI systems may develop better emotional intelligence capabilities, allowing them to assist leaders in understanding human behavior, negotiation, and conflict resolution.

While AI will become an indispensable tool for leaders, the essence of leadership will remain deeply human. Emotional intelligence, empathy, ethical reasoning, and vision are qualities that no AI system can fully replicate. The most effective leaders of the future will be those who harness AI's capabilities while maintaining a strong moral compass, creativity, and human-centered decision-making approach.

Conclusion

AI-powered leadership is transforming how decisions are made, offering unparalleled insights, predictive capabilities, and automation. By integrating AI into decision-making processes, leaders can enhance efficiency, mitigate risks, and drive innovation. However, ethical considerations, transparency, and the balance between AI and human judgment remain critical.

The future of leadership will not be about AI replacing human leaders but about creating a powerful synergy between artificial intelligence and human wisdom. Leaders who embrace AI while maintaining ethical responsibility and emotional intelligence will be the ones who shape the world of tomorrow.

Chapter 20: The Future of AI in Human-Centered Workplaces

As artificial intelligence continues to evolve, its role in the workplace is undergoing a profound transformation. AI is no longer just an automation tool for repetitive tasks; it is now an essential collaborator, enhancing human potential and creating more efficient, innovative, and adaptive workplaces. However, the future of AI in human-centered workplaces is not about replacing people—it is about augmenting their capabilities, fostering creativity, and improving work-life balance.

A human-centered workplace prioritizes employee well-being, values collaboration, and embraces AI as a supportive partner rather than a competitor. As organizations integrate AI, the focus must remain on ethical implementation, skill development, and the seamless blending of technology with human intuition and emotional intelligence.

AI as a Collaborative Partner in the Workplace

AI is shifting from being a mere productivity tool to becoming a true collaborator that works alongside humans. It enhances decision-making, improves efficiency, and enables employees to focus on meaningful and creative work.

1. **AI-Powered Personal Assistants**

2. Virtual AI assistants, such as chatbots and voice-activated systems, help employees manage schedules, organize tasks, and retrieve information instantly. These assistants can draft emails, schedule meetings, and even summarize documents, allowing workers to concentrate on high-priority tasks.

3. **AI in Knowledge Management**

AI-driven knowledge management systems help employees access relevant information quickly. By analyzing vast amounts of data, AI identifies patterns and provides insights, ensuring that employees have the resources they need to make informed decisions. AI can also facilitate seamless collaboration by suggesting relevant documents, experts, or teams based on work context.

4. AI in Problem-Solving and Innovation

By analyzing trends and suggesting solutions, AI plays a significant role in problem-solving and innovation. In industries such as engineering, design, and research, AI-driven simulations and predictive models allow employees to test ideas and optimize solutions before implementation.

5. AI and Human Creativity

Despite fears that AI will stifle creativity, it is proving to be an invaluable partner in creative industries. AI-generated ideas, designs, and content serve as inspiration, helping artists, writers, and designers explore new possibilities. AI tools in marketing, music composition, and content generation support human creativity rather than replace it.

AI in Workplace Efficiency and Productivity

AI is transforming how businesses operate by streamlining workflows and improving efficiency.

1. Smart Automation for Routine Tasks

AI-powered automation is reducing the burden of repetitive administrative work. In fields like HR, finance, and customer service, AI automates document processing, data entry, and routine queries, freeing employees to focus on strategic and interpersonal tasks.

2. Enhanced Communication and Collaboration

AI-driven translation and transcription tools break language barriers, making global collaboration easier. Real-time transcription services help employees record and review meetings, ensuring that important details are not lost.

3. AI-Powered Workflows

AI analyzes workflows to identify bottlenecks and suggest improvements. This optimization helps businesses allocate resources efficiently, reducing delays and increasing overall productivity.

AI and Employee Well-Being

A human-centered workplace prioritizes employee well-being, and AI is playing a growing role in supporting mental health and work-life balance.

1. AI in Employee Wellness Programs

AI-driven wellness applications track employee stress levels, suggest mindfulness exercises, and provide personalized health recommendations. Some companies use AI to monitor employee burnout risks by analyzing work patterns and suggesting breaks when necessary.

2. AI and Work-Life Balance

AI helps employees achieve a better work-life balance by optimizing schedules, automating mundane tasks, and ensuring workloads are evenly distributed. Smart scheduling systems allow employees to manage their time more effectively, reducing stress and improving job satisfaction.

3. AI in Diversity and Inclusion

AI tools can help organizations build more inclusive workplaces by removing biases in hiring and promotions. AI-driven recruitment platforms analyze resumes objectively, ensuring that hiring decisions are based on skills rather than unconscious biases.

Ethical Challenges of AI in the Workplace

As AI becomes more integrated into human-centered workplaces, ethical concerns must be addressed to ensure fair, responsible, and transparent implementation.

1. AI and Job Displacement

One of the biggest concerns about AI in the workplace is job displacement. While AI automates repetitive tasks, it also creates new job opportunities that require human skills. Organizations must invest in retraining programs to help employees transition into roles that leverage their creativity, emotional intelligence, and problem-solving abilities.

2. Privacy and Data Security

AI systems collect vast amounts of employee data to improve productivity and wellness. However, this raises privacy concerns. Companies must implement strict data protection measures and ensure transparency about how AI collects and uses employee information.

3. AI Decision-Making Transparency

AI-driven decisions in hiring, promotions, and performance evaluations must be transparent and explainable. Organizations should adopt explainable AI

(XAI) to ensure that employees understand how AI arrives at conclusions and to prevent biases.

The Future: A Synergistic Relationship Between AI and Humans

The future of AI in workplaces will not be about machines taking over human roles but about a synergistic relationship where AI enhances human potential.

1. AI and Lifelong Learning

AI will play a key role in upskilling employees, providing personalized learning experiences, and helping workers adapt to evolving job demands. AI-driven learning platforms will recommend courses, analyze skill gaps, and provide real-time feedback.

2. The Rise of Hybrid Teams

Workplaces of the future will have hybrid teams where AI works alongside human employees. AI will handle data-heavy tasks while humans focus on creativity, leadership, and emotional intelligence-driven interactions.

3. AI in Leadership and Management

AI will support leaders by providing insights into employee engagement, performance trends, and industry forecasts. However, human leadership qualities such as empathy, ethics, and vision will remain irreplaceable.

4. Human-Centered AI Design

Future AI systems will be designed with human needs in mind. AI interfaces will become more intuitive, adaptive, and responsive to human emotions, ensuring seamless collaboration between people and machines.

The future of AI in human-centered workplaces is one of collaboration, not competition. AI will enhance workplace efficiency, improve employee well-being, and foster innovation, but human qualities such as creativity, emotional intelligence, and ethical decision-making will remain indispensable. By designing AI with human needs in mind, organizations can create workplaces that are more inclusive, productive, and fulfilling for employees.

SECTION 5: AI in Science and Healthcare

Chapter 21: AI-Assisted Research: Revolutionizing Scientific Discoveries

Artificial intelligence is transforming scientific research at an unprecedented pace. From accelerating drug discovery to unraveling the mysteries of space, AI is revolutionizing how researchers analyze data, conduct experiments, and make groundbreaking discoveries. In the past, scientific progress was often limited by human capabilities—time-consuming calculations, limited data analysis tools, and the inability to process massive datasets. AI is breaking these barriers, enabling scientists to push the boundaries of knowledge faster and more efficiently than ever before.

By integrating AI into research, scientists can automate complex processes, detect hidden patterns in data, and generate insights that were once impossible to uncover. AI does not replace human ingenuity but acts as a powerful tool that amplifies human intellect, allowing researchers to focus on the most critical aspects of their work. This chapter explores the various ways AI is revolutionizing scientific discoveries and its profound impact on different fields of research.

AI in Data Analysis and Pattern Recognition

Scientific research often involves analyzing vast amounts of complex data. Traditionally, researchers relied on statistical models and manual computations, which were not only time-consuming but also prone to errors. AI-driven algorithms, particularly machine learning and deep learning, have transformed data analysis by identifying intricate patterns, correlations, and anomalies with remarkable accuracy.

1. **AI in Genomics and Bioinformatics**

2. AI has significantly advanced genomics, helping researchers decode the human genome at a faster pace than ever before. Machine learning models analyze genetic sequences to identify mutations linked to diseases, predict potential genetic disorders, and even assist in gene-editing techniques like CRISPR. AI-powered bioinformatics tools also help in sequencing DNA more efficiently, reducing research costs and time.

3. **AI in Climate Science**

Climate researchers rely on AI to analyze global weather patterns, predict natural disasters, and assess climate change impacts. Machine learning models process satellite imagery, temperature records, and oceanic data to identify long-term trends and provide accurate climate forecasts. AI-driven climate models help policymakers develop sustainable environmental policies.

4. **AI in Astrophysics**

Astronomers use AI to analyze vast amounts of astronomical data collected from space telescopes and radio observatories. AI helps identify exoplanets, detect gravitational waves, and even map dark matter distribution in the universe. With AI, researchers can process years' worth of data in hours, accelerating our understanding of the cosmos.

AI-Powered Drug Discovery and Medical Research

One of AI's most promising applications is in medical research, particularly in drug discovery. Developing a new drug typically takes years of experimentation, trials, and regulatory approvals. AI is revolutionizing this process by speeding up drug development, optimizing clinical trials, and predicting drug interactions.

1. **AI in Drug Discovery**

Pharmaceutical companies are using AI to analyze chemical compounds and predict their effectiveness against diseases. Machine learning models can screen thousands of potential drug molecules in a fraction of the time required by traditional methods. AI also helps in repurposing existing drugs for new treatments, as seen during the COVID-19 pandemic.

2. **AI in Disease Diagnosis and Treatment**

AI-powered diagnostic tools can analyze medical images, blood tests, and patient records to detect diseases at early stages. For example, AI-driven imaging systems are being used to identify cancerous tumors with greater accuracy than human radiologists. AI also assists in personalized medicine by tailoring treatments based on an individual's genetic profile.

3. AI in Epidemiology and Public Health

AI models help predict disease outbreaks by analyzing social media trends, travel patterns, and health records. During pandemics, AI has played a crucial role in tracking virus spread, optimizing vaccine distribution, and forecasting infection rates.

AI in Materials Science and Engineering

Material scientists are leveraging AI to discover new materials with enhanced properties for applications in energy, electronics, and manufacturing. Traditional materials research involved years of trial and error, but AI accelerates this process by predicting the properties of new materials before they are even synthesized.

1. AI in Nanotechnology

AI aids in the design and development of nanomaterials for medicine, electronics, and energy storage. Researchers use AI simulations to predict how nanoparticles interact with biological systems, leading to breakthroughs in targeted drug delivery and cancer treatment.

2. AI in Energy Research

AI is revolutionizing energy research by optimizing renewable energy sources, improving battery technology, and enhancing nuclear fusion experiments.

AI-driven simulations help scientists design more efficient solar panels, wind turbines, and energy storage systems.

3. AI in Quantum Computing Research

AI is playing a crucial role in the development of quantum computers, which have the potential to solve problems that classical computers cannot. Machine learning algorithms help optimize quantum circuits and correct errors in quantum computations.

AI in Social Sciences and Humanities Research

AI is not limited to hard sciences—it is also transforming research in social sciences, history, and humanities.

1. AI in Linguistics and Language Research

AI-powered natural language processing (NLP) models analyze language evolution, detect linguistic patterns, and even assist in language translation and preservation of endangered languages. AI tools are helping historians decipher ancient texts and scripts.

2. AI in Psychological Research

Psychologists use AI to analyze human behavior, predict mental health issues, and even develop AI-driven therapy applications. Sentiment analysis algorithms can assess emotional states based on social media activity, helping researchers understand public mental health trends.

3. AI in Economic and Political Research

Economists and political scientists use AI to analyze market trends, predict economic fluctuations, and assess political sentiments. AI-driven simulations help policymakers model the effects of economic policies before implementation.

Challenges and Ethical Considerations

While AI is revolutionizing scientific research, it also presents challenges and ethical concerns.

1. Bias in AI Models

AI algorithms are only as good as the data they are trained on. If the training data contains biases, AI models may produce skewed or misleading results. Ensuring diversity and accuracy in datasets is crucial for unbiased research.

2. Transparency and Explainability

Many AI-driven research models operate as "black boxes," meaning their decision-making processes are not easily interpretable. Scientists must develop explainable AI models to ensure transparency and reproducibility in research.

3. Data Privacy and Security

AI research relies on massive datasets, some of which include sensitive personal or medical information. Ensuring data privacy and compliance with regulations such as GDPR and HIPAA is essential for ethical AI implementation in research.

The Future of AI-Assisted Research

The future of AI in scientific research is promising, with advancements in computing power, data availability, and AI algorithms opening new frontiers in discovery.

1. AI and Interdisciplinary Research

AI will continue to bridge gaps between different fields of science, leading to interdisciplinary discoveries. For example, AI is already helping neuroscientists understand brain function by integrating insights from biology, physics, and computer science.

2. AI and Automated Scientific Discovery

AI-driven robotic laboratories and self-learning AI models will soon conduct experiments independently, making scientific discovery faster and more efficient.

Automated labs will be able to design, test, and refine experiments without human intervention.

3. AI in Space Exploration

AI will play a critical role in future space missions, from autonomous navigation of spacecraft to the discovery of extraterrestrial life. AI-driven analysis of Mars rovers' data is already helping scientists understand the planet's geology and climate.

AI is revolutionizing scientific research, making discoveries faster, more precise, and more impactful. From medicine to astrophysics, AI is enhancing human potential, helping researchers tackle complex challenges, and opening doors to new knowledge. However, responsible AI implementation is necessary to ensure ethical research practices, transparency, and fairness. As AI continues to evolve, it will not replace human curiosity and ingenuity but will serve as a powerful tool that amplifies our ability to explore, understand, and innovate.

Chapter 22: How AI is Transforming Drug Discovery and Medicine

Artificial intelligence is revolutionizing the field of medicine, particularly in drug discovery and healthcare. Traditionally, the process of developing new drugs is long, costly, and complex, often taking over a decade and billions of dollars to bring a single drug to market. However, AI is dramatically accelerating this process by analyzing massive datasets, predicting molecular interactions, and identifying potential treatments faster than human researchers ever could.

Beyond drug discovery, AI is transforming various aspects of medicine, from diagnosing diseases and personalizing treatments to predicting health outcomes and assisting in robotic surgeries. AI-powered systems are improving accuracy, efficiency, and accessibility in healthcare, leading to better patient outcomes and innovative solutions for previously incurable diseases. This chapter explores how AI is reshaping drug discovery and medicine, making healthcare more effective, affordable, and personalized.

AI in Drug Discovery

1. Accelerating Drug Discovery and Development

Traditionally, drug discovery involves extensive laboratory testing, trial-and-error experimentation, and complex clinical trials. AI has significantly reduced the time required for drug discovery by automating processes, analyzing vast biomedical datasets, and predicting the effectiveness of drug compounds with precision.

- **Molecular Screening and Drug Candidate Identification:** AI algorithms analyze billions of chemical compounds and their potential interactions with biological targets. Machine learning models can predict how molecules will bind to proteins, helping scientists identify promising drug candidates in a fraction of the time.
- **Repurposing Existing Drugs:** AI can analyze existing drugs to find new applications. For example, AI played a crucial role in identifying potential COVID-19 treatments by repurposing drugs like Remdesivir.
- **Reducing Costs:** By predicting which compounds are most likely to succeed in clinical trials, AI minimizes expensive failures and optimizes the drug development pipeline.

2. AI in Preclinical and Clinical Trials

Clinical trials are a crucial phase in drug development, but they are time-consuming and costly. AI is streamlining this process by improving patient recruitment, monitoring trial participants, and analyzing trial data more efficiently.

- **AI for Patient Selection:** AI analyzes patient data to identify suitable candidates for clinical trials, ensuring diverse and representative samples. This improves the success rate of trials by selecting participants who are most likely to respond to the treatment.

- **Real-Time Monitoring and Predictive Analysis:** AI-powered wearable devices and sensors track patients' health metrics during trials, allowing real-time data collection and immediate intervention if needed.
- **Optimizing Trial Design:** AI models simulate various trial designs and predict outcomes, helping researchers refine their methodologies for maximum effectiveness.

AI in Medical Diagnostics and Personalized Treatment

1. AI-Powered Disease Detection and Diagnosis

Medical diagnosis is one of the most critical applications of AI in healthcare. AI-driven diagnostic tools analyze medical images, genetic data, and patient records to detect diseases earlier and with higher accuracy than traditional methods.

- **AI in Radiology:** Deep learning algorithms analyze X-rays, MRIs, and CT scans to detect tumors, fractures, and abnormalities. AI-powered systems can identify early signs of cancer and other conditions with remarkable accuracy.

- **AI in Pathology:** AI assists pathologists by analyzing biopsy samples and detecting cancer cells at microscopic levels, improving early diagnosis and treatment planning.
- **AI in Ophthalmology and Cardiology:** AI-driven eye scans help detect diabetic retinopathy, glaucoma, and other vision-threatening diseases. Similarly, AI algorithms analyze ECG and heart scans to predict cardiovascular diseases before symptoms appear.

2. Personalized Medicine and AI-Driven Treatment Plans

Every individual's genetic makeup is different, which means that the same drug may not work equally well for everyone. AI is enabling **personalized medicine**, where treatments are tailored to each patient based on their genetic profile, lifestyle, and medical history.

- **Genomic Analysis for Precision Medicine:** AI analyzes genetic data to predict how a patient will respond to specific medications. This helps doctors prescribe the most effective treatments while minimizing side effects.
- **AI in Oncology:** AI assists oncologists in designing customized cancer treatments by

analyzing tumor DNA and predicting which
therapies will be most effective for a particular
patient.

- **Real-Time Health Monitoring and AI-Driven
  Interventions:** AI-powered wearables and smart
  devices track patients' health in real time,
  alerting doctors to potential issues before they
  become serious. For instance, AI-driven glucose
  monitors help diabetics maintain stable blood
  sugar levels.

AI in Drug Manufacturing and Supply Chain Management

1. AI-Optimized Drug Production

AI is revolutionizing pharmaceutical manufacturing by
improving efficiency, reducing waste, and ensuring
consistent quality.

- **AI-Driven Quality Control:** AI systems detect
  defects in drug formulations, ensuring high-
  quality production and reducing contamination
  risks.
- **Smart Manufacturing Systems:** AI optimizes
  production schedules, automates packaging
  processes, and predicts maintenance needs for
  pharmaceutical factories.

2. AI in Drug Distribution and Logistics

Ensuring that life-saving drugs reach patients in a timely manner is critical, and AI is improving the pharmaceutical supply chain by predicting demand and optimizing distribution.

- **AI-Powered Demand Forecasting:** AI analyzes prescription data, seasonal disease trends, and population health metrics to predict drug demand, preventing shortages and ensuring availability.
- **Automated Drug Dispensing and Distribution:** AI-powered robots and smart inventory systems are improving efficiency in pharmacies, hospitals, and drug distribution centers.

AI in Robotic Surgery and Assistive Technologies

1. AI in Robotic-Assisted Surgeries

AI-driven robotic systems are transforming surgery by enhancing precision, reducing human error, and improving patient outcomes.

- **Da Vinci Surgical System:** This AI-powered robotic system assists surgeons in performing minimally invasive procedures with greater accuracy and flexibility.

- **AI in Orthopedic and Neurosurgery:** AI helps design custom prosthetics, plan complex spinal surgeries, and guide surgeons with real-time feedback during procedures.

2. AI for Disability Support and Rehabilitation

AI is enhancing assistive technologies, improving the lives of individuals with disabilities and chronic conditions.

- **AI-Powered Prosthetics:** Smart prosthetic limbs use AI to adapt to a person's movement patterns, improving mobility and functionality.
- **AI in Speech and Hearing Aids:** AI-powered devices help people with hearing impairments by filtering background noise and enhancing speech recognition.

Challenges and Ethical Considerations in AI-Driven Medicine

Despite its transformative potential, AI in healthcare comes with challenges and ethical concerns that must be addressed.

1. Data Privacy and Security

AI relies on vast amounts of sensitive patient data, raising concerns about privacy, data breaches, and ethical use of personal health information. Strict regulations like HIPAA and GDPR must be enforced to protect patient confidentiality.

2. Algorithmic Bias and Inequality

AI models trained on biased data may produce inaccurate or discriminatory results. Efforts must be made to ensure AI systems are trained on diverse and representative datasets to prevent disparities in healthcare outcomes.

3. Human Oversight and the Role of Physicians

While AI enhances medical capabilities, it cannot replace human judgment and empathy. Doctors and healthcare professionals must oversee AI-driven decisions, ensuring that ethical considerations and patient welfare remain the top priority.

The Future of AI in Medicine

AI is set to play an even greater role in medicine in the coming decades. Future advancements will likely include:

- **AI-Generated Drug Design:** AI will design entirely new drugs, reducing reliance on trial-and-error methods.
- **AI-Powered Virtual Health Assistants:** AI chatbots and virtual assistants will provide instant medical advice, reducing the burden on healthcare professionals.
- **AI in Global Health:** AI will be used to address global health challenges, from predicting disease outbreaks to optimizing vaccine distribution in remote areas.

AI is revolutionizing drug discovery and medicine, accelerating the development of life-saving treatments, improving diagnostics, personalizing healthcare, and optimizing medical procedures. While challenges remain, the benefits of AI in healthcare are undeniable. As AI continues to evolve, it will enhance human expertise, making medicine more efficient, accessible, and effective in improving global health outcomes. AI is not replacing doctors—it is empowering them to save more lives and revolutionize healthcare for the better.

Chapter 23: The Role of AI in Precision Healthcare

Healthcare has traditionally followed a one-size-fits-all approach, where treatments and medications are designed for the average patient. However, every individual is unique, with distinct genetic, lifestyle, and environmental factors influencing their health. **Precision healthcare**—also known as personalized medicine—aims to tailor medical treatments to each individual, improving effectiveness and minimizing side effects.

Artificial Intelligence (AI) is at the forefront of this revolution, enabling precise diagnostics, targeted therapies, and customized healthcare plans. By analyzing vast amounts of genetic data, electronic health records, and real-time patient monitoring, AI helps doctors make data-driven decisions, ensuring that patients receive the right treatment at the right time. This chapter explores how AI is shaping precision healthcare, enhancing patient outcomes, and transforming the future of medicine.

AI-Driven Precision Diagnostics

1. AI in Medical Imaging and Disease Detection

Medical imaging is one of the most advanced applications of AI in precision healthcare. AI-powered systems analyze radiology scans, pathology slides, and medical images with high accuracy, enabling early disease detection and better treatment planning.

- **Cancer Detection:** AI-driven imaging tools can identify tumors in mammograms, lung scans, and MRIs earlier than human radiologists. These systems detect minute abnormalities that might be missed by the human eye, improving cancer survival rates.
- **Neurological Disorders:** AI is used to detect conditions like Alzheimer's, Parkinson's, and multiple sclerosis through brain imaging, enabling early intervention before severe symptoms develop.
- **Cardiovascular Diseases:** AI analyzes echocardiograms and angiograms to predict heart diseases, detect arterial blockages, and assess risks of heart attacks and strokes.

2. AI in Genetic and Molecular Analysis

AI is revolutionizing genomics, allowing scientists to decode DNA and predict disease risks with greater precision.

- **Genetic Risk Assessment:** AI analyzes genetic mutations linked to diseases like cancer, diabetes, and rare genetic disorders. This helps doctors offer preventive strategies tailored to an individual's genetic profile.
- **AI in Pharmacogenomics:** AI predicts how a patient's genes will respond to specific drugs,

ensuring that treatments are effective and reducing adverse drug reactions.

- **AI in Rare Disease Diagnosis:** AI systems analyze genomic data to identify rare diseases that are often misdiagnosed due to their complexity and rarity.

AI in Personalized Treatment and Therapy

1. AI-Powered Treatment Recommendations

AI helps doctors select the most effective treatment for individual patients by analyzing medical records, genetic data, and clinical trial results.

- **AI in Oncology:** AI-driven precision oncology tailors cancer treatments based on the genetic makeup of a tumor. For instance, AI helps determine whether a patient will respond better to chemotherapy, immunotherapy, or targeted gene therapy.
- **AI in Diabetes Management:** AI-driven insulin delivery systems adjust dosages in real time based on glucose levels, improving diabetes control and reducing complications.
- **AI in Mental Health Treatments:** AI-powered chatbots and digital therapeutics analyze speech patterns, social media activity, and

biometric data to personalize mental health interventions.

2. AI in Surgery and Robotics

AI-powered robotic systems assist surgeons in performing complex procedures with greater precision and fewer complications.

- **Minimally Invasive Surgeries:** AI-driven robotic systems, such as the Da Vinci surgical robot, allow surgeons to perform delicate procedures with enhanced dexterity and accuracy.
- **AI in Orthopedic Surgery:** AI models help plan joint replacements by analyzing patient-specific anatomical data, ensuring a perfect fit for implants.
- **AI in Neurosurgery:** AI assists neurosurgeons in mapping brain regions before surgery, reducing risks associated with brain procedures.

AI in Preventive Healthcare and Wellness

1. Predictive Analytics for Disease Prevention

AI uses predictive analytics to identify individuals at high risk for diseases, allowing preventive measures before symptoms appear.

- **AI in Cardiology:** AI models predict heart attack risks based on patient history, lifestyle, and genetic factors, enabling early interventions like diet changes or medication.
- **AI in Infectious Disease Prevention:** AI-powered epidemiology models track disease outbreaks and predict the spread of infections, helping governments and healthcare providers take timely action.
- **AI in Lifestyle Coaching:** AI-driven apps provide personalized health recommendations, such as fitness routines and dietary plans, based on individual biomarkers.

2. AI-Powered Wearables and Remote Monitoring

Wearable health devices and AI-powered remote monitoring tools allow continuous tracking of patients' vital signs, improving preventive care.

- **AI in Smartwatches and Fitness Trackers:** Devices like Apple Watch and Fitbit use AI to monitor heart rates, detect irregular rhythms, and alert users of potential health issues.
- **AI in Remote Patient Monitoring:** AI-powered sensors track blood pressure, oxygen levels, and glucose levels, sending real-time alerts to doctors for early intervention.

- **AI in Sleep Monitoring:** AI algorithms analyze sleep patterns and provide insights to improve sleep quality, reducing the risk of conditions like insomnia and sleep apnea.

AI in Precision Drug Development

1. AI for Drug Discovery and Personalized Medications

AI is accelerating drug discovery and enabling the creation of personalized medicines tailored to an individual's genetic profile.

- **AI-Designed Drugs:** AI models analyze billions of molecular structures to identify new drug candidates, significantly reducing drug development time.
- **AI in Gene Therapy:** AI helps design customized gene-editing treatments using CRISPR technology to target genetic disorders with high precision.
- **AI in Vaccine Development:** AI was instrumental in the rapid development of COVID-19 vaccines by analyzing viral genomes and predicting vaccine effectiveness.

2. AI in Drug Dosing and Administration

AI ensures that patients receive the right dosage of medication based on their metabolism, genetics, and lifestyle factors.

- **AI in Chemotherapy:** AI determines the optimal chemotherapy dosage for cancer patients, minimizing toxicity and side effects.
- **AI in Pain Management:** AI-powered pain management systems personalize opioid dosages to prevent addiction while ensuring pain relief.

Challenges and Ethical Considerations in AI-Driven Precision Healthcare

Despite its vast potential, AI in precision healthcare faces several challenges that must be addressed.

1. Data Privacy and Security

AI relies on large datasets containing sensitive patient information. Ensuring data privacy, preventing breaches, and complying with regulations like HIPAA and GDPR are critical concerns.

2. Bias and Fairness in AI Models

AI algorithms must be trained on diverse datasets to prevent bias in healthcare recommendations. A lack of diversity in training data can lead to inaccurate predictions, disproportionately affecting certain demographics.

3. Integration with Traditional Healthcare Systems

Implementing AI in hospitals and clinics requires seamless integration with existing electronic health record (EHR) systems. Standardizing AI adoption while maintaining physician oversight is essential for patient safety.

4. Ethical Decision-Making and AI's Role in Healthcare

AI should augment, not replace, human doctors. Ethical considerations must be addressed to ensure AI-driven healthcare remains patient-centered, with doctors making final decisions based on AI-generated insights.

The Future of AI in Precision Healthcare

The future of AI in precision healthcare is promising, with ongoing advancements expected to further revolutionize medicine.

- **AI-Generated Personalized Vaccines:** AI will create vaccines tailored to individuals based on their immune system responses.
- **AI-Driven Virtual Health Assistants:** AI-powered virtual doctors will provide real-time medical advice and remote consultations.
- **AI in Longevity and Anti-Aging Research:** AI will play a key role in developing treatments that slow aging and extend human lifespan.

AI is transforming precision healthcare by enabling accurate diagnostics, personalized treatments, predictive analytics, and drug discovery. It is shifting medicine from a reactive approach to a proactive and individualized model, improving patient outcomes and revolutionizing healthcare. While challenges remain, AI's integration with traditional medical practices will create a future where healthcare is more precise, accessible, and effective. AI is not replacing doctors—it is empowering them to deliver the best possible care tailored to each patient's unique needs.

Chapter 24: AI in Mental Health and Emotional Well-Being

Mental health is a critical aspect of overall well-being, yet it remains one of the most challenging areas of healthcare due to stigma, lack of resources, and the complexity of human emotions. Depression, anxiety, PTSD, and other mental health conditions affect millions worldwide, often going undiagnosed or untreated. Artificial Intelligence (AI) is now playing a transformative role in mental healthcare, offering new ways to diagnose, monitor, and support individuals struggling with mental health challenges.

AI-driven tools, including chatbots, virtual therapists, and emotion recognition systems, are helping bridge gaps in mental health services. From analyzing speech patterns to predicting emotional distress, AI is enabling early interventions and personalized treatment plans. This chapter explores how AI is reshaping mental health care, its benefits, limitations, and the ethical considerations surrounding its use.

AI in Mental Health Diagnosis and Early Detection

1. AI-Based Screening and Diagnostic Tools

AI is helping diagnose mental health conditions faster and more accurately than traditional methods.

- **Natural Language Processing (NLP):** AI analyzes speech patterns, word choice, and tone in conversations to detect signs of depression, anxiety, and other disorders. Studies have shown that AI can identify depressive symptoms based on subtle language cues, sometimes even before individuals recognize their symptoms.

- **Facial and Voice Emotion Analysis:** AI-driven emotion recognition software evaluates facial expressions, vocal tone, and body language to detect emotional distress. Companies like Affectiva and Amazon are developing AI tools that assess mood changes through voice modulation and facial movements.
- **Predictive Analytics for Suicide Prevention:** AI-powered algorithms analyze social media posts, text messages, and search histories to identify individuals at risk of suicide. Organizations like Crisis Text Line use AI to prioritize high-risk individuals and provide immediate support.

2. AI-Powered Wearables for Mental Health Monitoring

Smart devices and wearables equipped with AI technology continuously monitor physiological and behavioral patterns to detect signs of stress, anxiety, or depression.

- **Heart Rate and Sleep Tracking:** AI-powered wearables track sleep quality, heart rate variability, and stress levels to detect early signs of mental health issues.

- **Behavioral Pattern Analysis:** AI systems analyze daily routines, social interactions, and physical activity levels to identify patterns associated with declining mental health.
- **Real-Time Mood Monitoring:** Wearable devices can alert users to take breaks, meditate, or seek professional help when stress levels rise.

AI-Powered Virtual Therapists and Chatbots

1. AI Chatbots for Mental Health Support

AI-driven mental health chatbots provide immediate emotional support and therapy guidance, making mental health care more accessible.

- **Woebot:** A chatbot designed using cognitive-behavioral therapy (CBT) techniques, Woebot engages users in conversations to help manage stress, anxiety, and depression.
- **Wysa:** Another AI-driven chatbot that offers meditation exercises, mood tracking, and CBT-based self-help techniques.
- **Replika:** A chatbot that creates an empathetic AI friend for users to talk to, reducing feelings of loneliness and social isolation.

These AI chatbots provide 24/7 mental health support, helping individuals who may not have immediate access to therapists.

2. AI-Powered Virtual Therapy Sessions

AI is also enhancing traditional therapy by offering virtual therapy sessions with human-like AI therapists.

- **Automated Cognitive Behavioral Therapy (CBT):** AI-driven programs guide users through structured therapy sessions, offering exercises, personalized feedback, and progress tracking.
- **AI-Assisted Mindfulness and Meditation:** Apps like Headspace and Calm integrate AI to provide personalized meditation and relaxation techniques based on user stress levels.
- **AI for PTSD Treatment:** AI-powered virtual reality (VR) simulations help individuals with PTSD by recreating controlled environments to process traumatic experiences safely.

AI in Personalized Mental Health Treatment

1. AI-Driven Mental Health Apps

AI-powered apps are helping individuals manage their mental health with customized treatment plans and self-help tools.

- **Personalized Coping Strategies:** AI assesses an individual's emotional state and suggests coping mechanisms such as breathing exercises, journaling, or guided relaxation.
- **AI in Addiction Recovery:** AI-driven platforms like QuitGenius use machine learning to support individuals overcoming addiction by offering real-time encouragement and behavioral interventions.
- **AI in Stress Management:** AI-integrated apps analyze user behavior and provide stress management tips, such as recommending breaks, reducing screen time, or engaging in mindfulness exercises.

2. AI in Medication Management for Mental Health Disorders

AI is helping psychiatrists and patients optimize medication management for conditions like depression, bipolar disorder, and schizophrenia.

- **AI in Drug Response Prediction:** AI analyzes genetic and behavioral data to predict how an individual will respond to psychiatric medications, reducing trial-and-error prescriptions.
- **AI-Powered Pill Reminders:** AI-based apps send personalized reminders to take

medications, ensuring adherence to treatment plans.

- **AI in Side Effect Monitoring:** AI tracks patient-reported side effects, identifying patterns that help doctors adjust medication dosages or switch prescriptions.

AI in Workplace Mental Health and Employee Well-Being

1. AI-Powered Employee Wellness Programs

AI is transforming workplace mental health initiatives by providing personalized well-being programs.

- **AI-Driven Stress Management Tools:** AI monitors employee stress levels through biometric data and suggests relaxation techniques.
- **AI-Powered HR Chatbots:** AI chatbots assist employees with mental health concerns by offering confidential guidance and directing them to resources.
- **AI in Burnout Prevention:** AI systems analyze workload patterns and recommend schedule adjustments to prevent burnout.

2. AI in Work-Life Balance Optimization

AI helps organizations improve employee well-being by analyzing work habits and suggesting better work-life balance strategies.

- **AI in Meeting Scheduling:** AI assistants optimize meeting times to reduce stress and improve productivity.
- **AI in Digital Detox Recommendations:** AI tracks screen time and suggests breaks to prevent digital fatigue.
- **AI in Mental Health Policy Development:** AI analyzes employee feedback to help organizations design better mental health policies.

Challenges and Ethical Considerations in AI-Driven Mental Health

Despite its benefits, AI in mental health presents several challenges and ethical concerns.

1. Data Privacy and Confidentiality

Mental health data is highly sensitive, and AI-driven platforms must ensure that user conversations and health records remain private and secure.

2. Bias and Fairness in AI Models

AI models may inherit biases from training data, leading to inaccurate mental health assessments, especially for diverse populations. Ensuring diverse and inclusive training datasets is crucial.

3. The Limitations of AI in Understanding Human Emotions

While AI can detect emotional cues, it lacks true empathy and human intuition. AI should be used as a supplement to human therapists rather than a replacement.

4. Ethical Use of AI in Mental Health

AI-driven mental health tools must be designed with ethical guidelines to prevent misinformation, over-reliance on AI, and potential emotional harm to users.

The Future of AI in Mental Health and Emotional Well-Being

The future of AI in mental health looks promising, with continuous advancements expected to enhance emotional well-being support.

- **AI-Powered Emotional Intelligence Assistants:** AI will become better at recognizing and responding to human emotions in real-time, offering more meaningful mental health support.

- **AI in Trauma Recovery:** AI-driven virtual reality (VR) therapy will provide immersive experiences for trauma recovery and exposure therapy.
- **AI in Mental Health Crisis Response:** AI systems will be integrated into emergency response services to identify and assist individuals experiencing mental health crises.
- **AI in Neurotechnology:** AI-powered brain-computer interfaces (BCIs) will help individuals with severe mental health conditions by directly interacting with neural activity.

AI is revolutionizing mental health care by providing early diagnosis, virtual therapy, personalized treatment, and workplace well-being solutions. While AI cannot replace human therapists, it serves as a valuable tool to improve accessibility and support for mental health services. As technology evolves, AI-driven mental health solutions will continue to enhance emotional well-being, reduce stigma, and make mental healthcare more effective and inclusive. However, ensuring ethical AI use and maintaining the human touch in mental health care remains essential.

Chapter 25: Human Doctors vs. AI Diagnosis: A Symbiotic Relationship

The field of medicine has always been driven by advancements in technology, from the discovery of X-rays to robotic-assisted surgeries. However, the introduction of Artificial Intelligence (AI) in healthcare has sparked a critical debate: Will AI eventually replace human doctors, or will it serve as an invaluable tool to enhance medical practice? The reality is that AI is not a replacement but a partner—one that complements human expertise rather than competing with it.

The Strengths of AI in Diagnosis

AI has revolutionized medical diagnostics by processing vast amounts of data faster and more accurately than human doctors. Machine learning algorithms can analyze medical images, detect early signs of diseases like cancer, and predict health risks based on genetic information. For example, AI-powered radiology tools can identify abnormalities in X-rays and MRIs with remarkable precision, sometimes surpassing human radiologists in speed and accuracy.

AI also plays a crucial role in analyzing patient histories and lab results to detect patterns that might go unnoticed by a human doctor. Predictive analytics can help identify early warning signs of chronic diseases like diabetes or heart disease, allowing for proactive intervention. Additionally, AI chatbots and virtual assistants provide preliminary symptom analysis, helping patients determine whether they need immediate medical attention.

The Irreplaceable Role of Human Doctors

Despite AI's impressive capabilities, it lacks fundamental human qualities that are essential in medical practice. One of the most critical aspects of healthcare is emotional intelligence—something AI cannot replicate. A doctor's ability to communicate with empathy, understand a patient's fears, and provide reassurance plays a significant role in the healing process.

Medical decisions are often complex and require ethical judgment, something AI is not equipped to handle. For example, in cases where a treatment has potential risks, a doctor must consider the patient's preferences, cultural background, and psychological state before making a recommendation. AI can provide data-driven insights, but it is ultimately the human doctor who interprets and applies them in a way that aligns with the patient's unique needs.

Moreover, AI is only as good as the data it is trained on. If an AI system is exposed to biased or incomplete data, it can lead to incorrect diagnoses. Human doctors bring experience, intuition, and clinical reasoning that allow them to question AI-generated results when something seems off. This ability to integrate data with real-world experience makes doctors indispensable.

A Powerful Partnership for the Future

Rather than replacing doctors, AI is best utilized as an assistant that enhances medical decision-making. The most promising healthcare systems of the future will integrate AI into routine diagnostics while keeping doctors at the center of patient care. AI can handle time-consuming tasks like analyzing test results, freeing doctors to focus on patient interaction and treatment planning.

For instance, AI can streamline workflows in hospitals by predicting patient deterioration, optimizing resource allocation, and reducing administrative burdens. Telemedicine, powered by AI, can provide faster consultations and assist doctors in remote areas where specialized care is limited.

By working together, AI and human doctors can provide faster, more accurate, and more personalized healthcare. AI offers efficiency and data-driven insights, while human doctors bring compassion, judgment, and holistic understanding. The key to the future of medicine is not AI or doctors alone but a well-balanced collaboration where technology enhances, rather than replaces, human expertise.

The future of healthcare lies in a symbiotic relationship between AI and human doctors. AI will continue to revolutionize diagnostics and data analysis, but the human touch will remain irreplaceable in-patient care. Rather than fearing AI's rise in medicine, we should embrace it as a powerful ally that helps doctors provide better, faster, and more precise healthcare. In this partnership, both AI and human intelligence thrive—ensuring the best possible outcomes for patients worldwide.

Chapter 25. Human Doctors vs. AI Diagnosis: A Symbiotic Relationship

The intersection of artificial intelligence (AI) and medicine is revolutionizing healthcare, particularly in the realm of diagnosis. AI-powered systems are capable of analyzing vast amounts of medical data, identifying patterns, and making diagnostic predictions with remarkable accuracy. However, human doctors bring irreplaceable qualities such as experience, empathy, ethical reasoning, and contextual understanding to patient care. Rather than replacing doctors, AI serves as a powerful tool to enhance diagnostic precision, improve efficiency, and support clinical decision-making. This chapter explores the evolving relationship between AI and human doctors, highlighting how they complement each other in modern healthcare.

The Strengths of AI in Diagnosis

1. Speed and Efficiency

AI systems can process medical data, including lab results, imaging scans, and patient histories, at speeds far beyond human capability. Algorithms trained on extensive datasets can quickly detect abnormalities in medical images, flagging potential concerns for further investigation. For example, AI-driven radiology tools can analyze thousands of X-rays, MRIs, and CT scans within seconds, significantly reducing diagnostic turnaround time.

2. Accuracy and Consistency

AI has shown impressive accuracy in diagnosing diseases, sometimes outperforming human specialists in specific areas. Studies have demonstrated that AI can detect conditions like diabetic retinopathy, breast cancer, and lung nodules with precision comparable to or even exceeding that of experienced doctors. Unlike humans, AI does not suffer from fatigue or cognitive biases, ensuring consistency in diagnoses across cases.

3. Early Detection and Predictive Analysis

AI excels at identifying subtle patterns in data that may be overlooked by the human eye. Predictive analytics powered by AI can detect early signs of diseases such as cancer, Alzheimer's, and cardiovascular conditions before symptoms manifest. By analyzing genetic markers, lifestyle factors, and historical patient data, AI can help identify individuals at high risk and enable early intervention strategies.

4. Handling Large-Scale Data and Rare Diseases

With the explosion of medical data, AI is instrumental in managing and analyzing vast datasets to uncover insights that would be challenging for human doctors alone. AI is particularly useful in diagnosing rare diseases by cross-referencing symptoms and genetic information with global databases, ensuring patients receive accurate diagnoses even for conditions that are uncommon in a particular region.

The Irreplaceable Role of Human Doctors

1. Clinical Judgment and Contextual Understanding

While AI excels at pattern recognition and data processing, human doctors apply clinical reasoning, taking into account a patient's history, lifestyle, and external factors that AI may not fully comprehend. A doctor's ability to consider social, emotional, and psychological aspects of a patient's condition ensures a more holistic approach to diagnosis and treatment.

2. Empathy and Doctor-Patient Relationship

A critical component of healthcare is the human connection between doctors and patients. AI lacks empathy, compassion, and the ability to provide emotional support. Doctors build trust with patients, communicate diagnoses with sensitivity, and guide them through treatment decisions. In fields such as oncology and palliative care, the human touch remains irreplaceable.

3. Ethical and Moral Decision-Making

Medical decisions often involve ethical dilemmas, such as end-of-life care, organ transplants, or treatment prioritization in resource-limited settings. While AI can provide data-driven recommendations, doctors must weigh ethical considerations, cultural values, and patient preferences when making final decisions. Human judgment ensures that medical care aligns with both ethical principles and individual patient needs.

4. Personalized Care and Treatment Adaptation

Every patient is unique, and treatment plans must be tailored accordingly. AI provides recommendations based on algorithms, but doctors must interpret these suggestions within the broader context of a patient's condition, lifestyle, and response to treatment. Adjusting medication dosages, considering side effects, and making real-time treatment modifications require a level of adaptability that AI cannot independently provide.

The Symbiotic Relationship: AI and Doctors Working Together

Rather than replacing doctors, AI acts as an invaluable assistant, enhancing the efficiency and accuracy of medical practice. The ideal healthcare system leverages AI's computational power while preserving the human elements of medicine. Here's how AI and doctors work together:

1. AI as a Diagnostic Assistant

AI assists doctors by providing second opinions, flagging potential misdiagnoses, and offering data-driven insights. In radiology, AI highlights suspicious areas in scans, which doctors then evaluate for final diagnosis. This collaboration minimizes errors and ensures that subtle abnormalities are not overlooked.

2. AI in Decision Support Systems

AI-driven clinical decision support systems (CDSS) help doctors make informed choices by analyzing medical records, lab results, and research studies. These systems provide evidence-based recommendations, helping doctors choose the most effective treatment plans while considering the latest medical advancements.

3. AI in Workflow Optimization

AI streamlines administrative tasks such as medical documentation, scheduling, and electronic health record management. This allows doctors to focus more on patient care rather than being burdened by paperwork. AI-driven voice recognition tools transcribe patient interactions, reducing the time spent on documentation.

4. AI in Medical Training and Continuous Learning

AI-powered platforms provide medical students and professionals with real-time learning opportunities. Virtual simulations and AI-based diagnostic tools enhance medical education by exposing doctors to diverse cases and rare conditions, improving their diagnostic skills.

Challenges and Ethical Considerations

Despite the advantages of AI in healthcare, several challenges and ethical concerns must be addressed:

1. Data Privacy and Security

AI relies on vast amounts of patient data, raising concerns about data security, privacy breaches, and unauthorized access. Ensuring compliance with health regulations such as HIPAA and GDPR is crucial to maintaining patient trust.

2. AI Bias and Algorithmic Limitations

AI models are only as good as the data they are trained on. If training data lacks diversity, AI can produce biased diagnoses, disproportionately affecting certain populations. Ensuring unbiased datasets and continuous algorithm refinement is essential for equitable healthcare outcomes.

3. Over-Reliance on AI

While AI enhances diagnostic accuracy, over-reliance on technology without human verification can lead to errors. Doctors must critically evaluate AI recommendations rather than blindly accepting algorithmic conclusions.

4. Ethical Use of AI in Patient Care

Decisions about AI's role in patient care must be made with caution. Patients should have the right to know when AI is involved in their diagnosis and treatment. Transparency and accountability are essential in ensuring AI is used responsibly.

The Future of AI and Human Doctors in Healthcare

The future of medicine lies in a collaborative model where AI augments human expertise rather than replacing it. Innovations such as AI-driven personalized medicine, robotic-assisted surgeries, and AI-powered drug discovery will continue to reshape healthcare. However, human doctors will remain central to patient care, providing empathy, ethical judgment, and clinical expertise.

As AI continues to evolve, medical professionals must embrace technological advancements while maintaining the human touch that defines healthcare. A balanced approach, where AI serves as a supportive tool while doctors lead patient interactions, will ensure the best possible outcomes in diagnosis, treatment, and overall patient well-being.

The relationship between AI and human doctors is not a competition but a partnership. AI enhances diagnostic accuracy, speeds up processes, and provides valuable insights, but it cannot replace the empathy, ethical reasoning, and personalized care that human doctors provide. The future of healthcare lies in a symbiotic relationship where AI supports doctors in delivering faster, more precise, and more compassionate medical care. By combining technological advancements with human expertise, we can create a healthcare system that is both efficient and patient-centered, ensuring better outcomes for all.

SECTION 6: AI in Education and Learning

Chapter 26. AI as a Teacher: Strengthening Human Learning

Education has always evolved with technological advancements, from the printing press to digital learning tools. Today, artificial intelligence (AI) is revolutionizing the way people learn, offering personalized instruction, real-time feedback, and adaptive learning experiences. While AI cannot replace human teachers, it serves as a powerful tool to enhance education by making learning more efficient, engaging, and accessible. This chapter explores how AI is transforming education, its strengths and limitations, and the future of AI-powered learning.

The Role of AI in Education

AI has emerged as a game-changer in education, offering innovative ways to support both students and teachers. Unlike traditional teaching methods, AI-driven learning platforms can adapt to individual learning styles, pace, and preferences, ensuring that students receive tailored instruction. AI is used in various educational settings, from online courses and tutoring programs to classrooms and corporate training environments.

How AI Enhances Learning

1. Personalized Learning Experiences

One of AI's greatest strengths in education is its ability to personalize learning. AI-powered platforms analyze students' strengths, weaknesses, and learning habits to create customized lesson plans. Adaptive learning systems adjust content in real time, ensuring that students receive materials at their appropriate skill level. This approach is especially useful for subjects like mathematics and language learning, where students progress at different speeds.

2. Intelligent Tutoring Systems (ITS)

AI-driven tutoring systems provide real-time feedback and support, mimicking the role of a personal tutor. These systems can answer student queries, explain complex concepts, and suggest additional resources. Unlike human tutors, AI tutors are available 24/7, making learning more accessible to students regardless of their location or schedule.

3. Automated Grading and Assessment

AI streamlines the grading process by automatically evaluating assignments, quizzes, and exams. This reduces teachers' workload and provides students with instant feedback, allowing them to learn from their mistakes and improve. AI-driven assessments can also analyze writing patterns and grammar, offering detailed corrections and suggestions for improvement.

4. Enhancing Engagement with Interactive Learning

AI makes learning more engaging through gamification, interactive simulations, and virtual reality. AI-powered platforms use storytelling, challenges, and rewards to keep students motivated. Virtual labs and simulations allow students to conduct experiments in a safe, controlled environment, making subjects like physics, chemistry, and biology more interactive.

5. Language Learning and AI-Powered Translation

Language learning apps like Duolingo and Google Translate use AI to provide instant translations, pronunciation corrections, and grammar suggestions. AI can analyze speech patterns and offer real-time feedback, helping learners improve their language skills. This is particularly beneficial for students learning new languages without direct access to native speakers.

6. AI for Special Education

AI plays a crucial role in supporting students with disabilities by providing assistive technologies such as speech-to-text, text-to-speech, and predictive text tools. AI-powered learning applications cater to students with dyslexia, visual impairments, and other learning challenges, ensuring that education is inclusive and accessible to all.

7. Virtual Classrooms and AI-Powered Teaching Assistants

With the rise of online education, AI-driven virtual classrooms are becoming more common. AI teaching assistants help manage class discussions, answer frequently asked questions, and provide personalized support to students. Platforms like Coursera, Khan Academy, and edX integrate AI to improve user experience, track progress, and recommend relevant courses.

The Role of Human Teachers in AI-Powered Education

While AI is transforming education, it cannot replace human teachers. The role of educators remains essential in guiding students, fostering creativity, and developing critical thinking skills. AI can handle repetitive tasks and provide instant feedback, but teachers bring emotional intelligence, mentorship, and real-world experience to the classroom.

1. Emotional and Social Development

Education is not just about acquiring knowledge; it also involves emotional and social growth. Teachers help students develop communication skills, teamwork, and empathy—qualities that AI lacks. A human teacher understands the emotional needs of students, offering support and encouragement that AI cannot replicate.

2. Critical Thinking and Creativity

AI excels at delivering structured knowledge, but it struggles with fostering creativity and critical thinking. Teachers encourage students to question, analyze, and think independently. They create an environment where students can engage in debates, explore new ideas, and develop problem-solving skills.

3. Ethical and Moral Guidance

Education involves more than just academic subjects; it also includes ethical and moral teachings. Teachers help students navigate complex moral dilemmas, discuss societal issues, and understand cultural values. AI, on the other hand, lacks moral reasoning and cannot replace the ethical guidance provided by human educators.

4. Customizing Learning Beyond Algorithms

While AI personalizes learning based on data, teachers provide a deeper level of customization by considering students' emotions, interests, and personal backgrounds. A teacher can recognize when a student is struggling due to non-academic reasons, such as personal challenges, and offer appropriate support.

Challenges and Ethical Considerations

Despite its many advantages, the integration of AI in education also presents challenges and ethical concerns.

1. Data Privacy and Security

AI-powered learning platforms collect vast amounts of student data, raising concerns about privacy and security. It is essential to ensure that student information is protected and used responsibly.

2. AI Bias and Fairness

AI algorithms can inherit biases from their training data, leading to unfair treatment of students from diverse backgrounds. Developers must ensure that AI models are trained on diverse datasets to promote fairness and inclusivity in education.

3. Over-Reliance on AI

While AI enhances education, relying too much on technology can lead to reduced human interaction and a lack of essential soft skills. A balanced approach is necessary to ensure that AI complements, rather than replaces, traditional teaching methods.

4. Accessibility and the Digital Divide

AI-powered education requires access to technology and the internet, which is not equally available to all students. Bridging the digital divide is crucial to ensuring that AI-driven learning benefits students from all socioeconomic backgrounds.

The Future of AI in Education

AI's role in education will continue to expand, making learning more personalized, efficient, and accessible. Future advancements may include AI-driven lifelong learning programs, virtual reality classrooms, and AI-powered mentorship programs. As AI continues to evolve, the key will be finding the right balance between technology and human interaction.

The future of education lies in a hybrid model where AI supports teachers by automating administrative tasks, enhancing personalized learning, and providing valuable insights. However, human educators will remain at the core of education, ensuring that learning is not just about acquiring knowledge but also about developing emotional intelligence, creativity, and ethical reasoning.

AI is transforming education by providing personalized learning, real-time feedback, and interactive experiences. It enhances efficiency, accessibility, and engagement, making learning more effective. However, AI cannot replace the human touch that teachers bring to education. Emotional intelligence, creativity, ethical reasoning, and mentorship are areas where human teachers excel. The future of education will be a collaborative effort between AI and human educators, creating a learning environment that is both technologically advanced and deeply human-centered. By leveraging the strengths of AI while preserving the essential role of teachers, we can create a more inclusive, engaging, and effective educational system.

Chapter 27. AI in Personalized Education and Skill Development

The traditional education system follows a one-size-fits-all approach, often failing to cater to individual learning needs. With artificial intelligence (AI), personalized education has become a reality, enabling students and professionals to acquire knowledge and skills at their own pace. AI-driven educational platforms analyze user behavior, learning styles, and progress to create customized learning experiences. This chapter explores how AI enhances personalized education, facilitates skill development, and prepares individuals for a rapidly evolving job market.

How AI Personalizes Education

1. Adaptive Learning Systems

AI-powered adaptive learning systems tailor educational content to the learner's needs. These platforms track student performance in real time, adjusting the difficulty level and recommending relevant resources based on progress. For example, if a student struggles with a particular math concept, the system will provide additional exercises and explanations before moving forward. This personalized approach ensures that learners grasp concepts thoroughly before advancing.

2. AI-Powered Tutoring and Virtual Instructors

AI-driven tutoring systems serve as virtual instructors, providing instant feedback and guidance. Unlike traditional classroom settings where teachers have limited time for individual students, AI tutors offer 24/7 assistance. These systems answer queries, assess performance, and suggest improvement strategies. Platforms like Khan Academy, Duolingo, and Coursera use AI to enhance learning experiences.

3. Customized Learning Paths

AI creates personalized learning paths based on a student's interests, goals, and skill levels. For instance, an aspiring data scientist might receive a curated course sequence covering Python, machine learning, and data visualization. AI ensures that learners focus on relevant topics, avoiding unnecessary repetition while reinforcing weaker areas.

4. Smart Content Creation

AI can generate and structure educational content, making it more engaging and efficient. Smart content includes:

- **Interactive textbooks** that adapt based on student responses.
- **AI-generated quizzes** that test knowledge and provide instant feedback.
- **Summarized learning materials** that condense vast information into digestible formats.

These innovations make studying more interactive and accessible.

AI in Skill Development

1. Personalized Career Development

AI-driven career guidance tools help individuals identify suitable career paths based on their strengths and interests. Platforms like LinkedIn Learning and Coursera recommend skill-building courses aligned with market demands. AI assists professionals in staying competitive by suggesting relevant certifications and learning resources.

2. AI in Corporate Training

Organizations use AI to design employee training programs that enhance skills and productivity. AI-powered learning management systems assess employee performance and recommend training modules that align with job roles. This targeted approach improves efficiency and ensures continuous professional development.

3. Gamification and Interactive Learning

AI incorporates gamification elements into skill development, making learning more engaging. AI-powered simulations, virtual labs, and real-world scenarios help learners apply knowledge in practical settings. For example, flight simulators train pilots using AI-driven scenarios, while medical students practice surgeries in virtual environments.

4. Language Learning and AI Assistance

AI-powered tools like Duolingo, Google Translate, and Grammarly assist in language learning and communication skills. AI provides real-time pronunciation feedback, grammar suggestions, and language translation, making it easier for learners to master new languages.

The Benefits of AI-Driven Personalized Learning

1. **Efficiency** – AI streamlines learning, ensuring students focus on essential topics.
2. **Accessibility** – AI-powered platforms provide learning opportunities to people in remote areas.
3. **Flexibility** – Learners can access courses anytime, anywhere, at their own pace.
4. **Engagement** – Interactive and adaptive content keeps learners motivated.
5. **Continuous Improvement** – AI provides real-time feedback, allowing learners to refine their skills.

Challenges and Ethical Considerations

Despite its advantages, AI-driven personalized education comes with challenges:

1. **Data Privacy Concerns** – AI collects vast amounts of user data, raising privacy and security issues.
2. **Digital Divide** – Not all learners have access to AI-powered education due to financial or technological barriers.
3. **Over-Reliance on AI** – Human mentorship remains essential in education, as AI cannot

replace emotional intelligence and critical thinking guidance.

The Future of AI in Education and Skill Development

AI will continue to revolutionize education by integrating augmented reality (AR), virtual reality (VR), and blockchain-based credentialing. AI-powered learning companions will become more advanced, offering hyper-personalized learning experiences. As AI evolves, the goal should be to complement, not replace, human educators, ensuring that personalized learning remains effective, ethical, and inclusive.

AI is transforming education and skill development by providing personalized learning experiences, adaptive tutoring, and career guidance. It enhances accessibility, engagement, and efficiency, empowering individuals to acquire knowledge and stay competitive in a dynamic world. However, the role of human educators remains crucial in fostering creativity, emotional intelligence, and ethical reasoning. The future of AI in education lies in collaboration— leveraging AI's capabilities while preserving the human touch in learning and skill development.

Chapter 28. The Future of AI in Schools and Universities

Artificial intelligence (AI) is reshaping education, from primary schools to prestigious universities. As AI continues to evolve, its role in classrooms will extend beyond simple automation to becoming an integral part of personalized learning, administrative efficiency, and innovative teaching methods. While traditional education has remained largely unchanged for centuries, AI promises to revolutionize how students learn, how teachers instruct, and how institutions operate. This chapter explores the transformative impact of AI in schools and universities, its benefits, challenges, and the future of AI-driven education.

AI-Powered Personalized Learning

One of AI's most significant contributions to education is personalized learning. Unlike conventional teaching, which follows a uniform curriculum, AI enables adaptive learning that caters to each student's needs.

1. **Intelligent Tutoring Systems (ITS):** AI-driven tutoring platforms analyze students' strengths and weaknesses, offering customized exercises and feedback. Systems like Carnegie Learning and Squirrel AI provide real-time guidance, making learning more effective.

2. **Adaptive Learning Platforms:** AI tailors' coursework and assessments based on student performance, ensuring a more efficient and engaging educational experience. These systems help slow learners reinforce foundational concepts while allowing advanced students to move ahead at their own pace.
3. **Language and Writing Assistance:** AI-powered tools like Grammarly and Google's AI-based language assistants provide students with grammar correction, writing suggestions, and even automated essay grading, improving literacy and communication skills.

AI in Teaching and Classroom Management

AI enhances the teaching experience by reducing administrative burdens and enabling educators to focus on creative and interactive teaching methods.

1. **AI-Powered Lesson Planning:** AI assists teachers in designing lesson plans by analyzing vast amounts of educational data. It recommends optimal teaching strategies, multimedia resources, and assignments tailored to specific topics.
2. **Automated Grading and Assessment:** AI streamlines the grading process, providing instant feedback on quizzes, assignments, and

even complex essays. This allows teachers to focus on mentoring students rather than spending hours evaluating test papers.

3. **Virtual Classrooms and AI Teaching Assistants:** AI-powered chatbots and virtual assistants help answer students' questions, facilitate discussions, and provide additional learning resources, making online and hybrid learning more interactive.

AI in Universities: Research and Innovation

At the university level, AI is revolutionizing research and innovation by accelerating data analysis and expanding the possibilities of scientific discovery.

1. **AI in Academic Research:** AI assists researchers in sorting through vast datasets, identifying patterns, and making predictions. Fields such as medicine, physics, and social sciences benefit from AI's ability to process complex data efficiently.

2. **AI in Career Guidance and Student Counseling:** AI-driven career guidance systems analyze students' skills, interests, and job market trends to recommend the best academic and career paths. This helps students make informed decisions about their future.

3. **AI-Powered University Administration:** AI optimizes various administrative tasks, including enrollment management, scheduling, and student record-keeping, improving institutional efficiency.

The Ethical and Social Challenges of AI in Education

Despite its advantages, integrating AI in education presents challenges and ethical concerns:

1. **Data Privacy and Security:** AI-driven learning platforms collect massive amounts of student data. Ensuring data protection and ethical AI usage is crucial to maintaining trust in AI-driven education.
2. **Equity and Accessibility:** While AI has the potential to democratize education, the digital divide remains a concern. Not all students have equal access to AI-powered learning tools, which could widen educational inequalities.
3. **Over-Reliance on AI:** While AI enhances learning, it cannot replace human teachers' emotional intelligence, mentorship, and critical thinking guidance. Striking a balance between AI assistance and human instruction is essential.

The Future of AI in Schools and Universities

The future of AI in education is promising, with several advancements expected:

1. **AI-Powered Immersive Learning:** Virtual reality (VR) and augmented reality (AR) combined with AI will create interactive and immersive learning environments, enhancing subjects like history, science, and engineering.
2. **Lifelong Learning and AI:** AI will support continuous education by recommending personalized learning paths for professionals seeking skill upgrades and career transitions.
3. **AI-Powered Global Classrooms:** AI translation tools will break language barriers, allowing students worldwide to access quality education in their native languages.

AI is poised to transform education by making learning more personalized, efficient, and accessible. While challenges remain, the integration of AI in schools and universities will enhance teaching methods, streamline administration, and revolutionize research. However, the future of AI in education should be one of collaboration—where AI complements human educators rather than replacing them. By harnessing AI responsibly, we can create a future where education is more inclusive, innovative, and impactful.

Chapter 29. AI's Role in Lifelong Learning and Career Growth

In today's fast-paced world, learning doesn't stop after formal education. Continuous skill development is essential to staying relevant in an ever-evolving job market. Artificial intelligence (AI) is revolutionizing lifelong learning and career growth by offering personalized learning experiences, automating skill development, and predicting industry trends. With AI-powered tools, individuals can learn at their own pace, receive tailored recommendations, and stay competitive in their careers. This chapter explores how AI is transforming lifelong learning and professional development.

AI-Powered Personalized Learning

One of AI's most significant contributions to lifelong learning is its ability to tailor educational content to individual needs. Unlike traditional one-size-fits-all education, AI adapts to a learner's progress and preferences.

1. **Adaptive Learning Platforms:** AI-driven platforms such as Coursera, Udemy, and LinkedIn Learning customize learning paths based on users' skills, interests, and career

goals. These platforms use algorithms to recommend courses, suggest exercises, and provide real-time feedback.

2. **Microlearning and AI-Assisted Content Curation:** AI breaks complex subjects into bite-sized lessons, making it easier for professionals to learn on the go. AI curates the most relevant articles, videos, and courses to ensure learners get high-quality content without information overload.

3. **AI-Powered Virtual Tutors:** AI-driven chatbots and virtual tutors provide instant clarification on complex topics, enabling users to grasp difficult concepts without waiting for human instructors.

AI in Career Development and Job Market Insights

AI is not just enhancing education; it is also transforming career growth by offering data-driven insights into job market trends and skill demands.

1. **AI-Powered Career Guidance:** Platforms like IBM Watson Career Coach analyze a professional's skills, experience, and aspirations to suggest the best career paths. AI can assess job market trends and recommend skill upgrades based on future industry needs.

2. **Predicting Industry Trends:** AI analyzes vast amounts of job market data to identify emerging careers and declining industries. This helps professionals stay ahead by acquiring skills that will be in demand in the future.
3. **Resume Optimization and Job Matching:** AI-driven platforms like LinkedIn and Indeed use machine learning to match job seekers with relevant opportunities, helping candidates tailor their resumes and applications for specific roles.

AI in Professional Skill Development

In an era where automation is reshaping industries, continuous skill development is critical. AI helps professionals stay ahead by facilitating upskilling and reskilling.

1. **AI in Corporate Training:** Companies use AI-powered platforms to train employees on new technologies, workplace policies, and leadership skills. AI identifies skill gaps and recommends personalized training modules.
2. **AI in Soft Skills Training:** AI-powered simulations and virtual mentors help individuals improve communication, negotiation, and leadership skills, which are crucial for career advancement.

3. **Real-Time Feedback and Performance Assessment:** AI provides real-time feedback during online courses, helping learners identify weaknesses and improve efficiency. Gamification techniques powered by AI make learning engaging and interactive.

AI and the Gig Economy

AI is playing a pivotal role in shaping the gig economy by enabling freelancers and independent workers to stay competitive.

1. **AI-Powered Project Matching:** Platforms like Upwork and Fiverr use AI to connect freelancers with suitable projects based on their skills, experience, and previous work history.
2. **AI-Driven Pricing and Market Insights:** Freelancers can use AI tools to analyze market rates for their services, helping them price their work competitively.
3. **AI in Continuous Skill Building:** Gig workers often need to adapt quickly to new technologies. AI-driven platforms suggest relevant courses and certifications based on industry trends.

Challenges and Ethical Considerations

While AI is transforming lifelong learning and career growth, some challenges and ethical concerns must be addressed.

1. **Data Privacy and Security:** AI-powered learning and career platforms collect vast amounts of personal data. Ensuring that this data is protected and used ethically is critical.
2. **Bias in AI Algorithms:** AI-based hiring and training platforms must be designed to avoid biases that could disadvantage certain groups of learners or job seekers.
3. **Human-AI Balance in Learning:** While AI enhances learning, human mentors, teachers, and career coaches remain irreplaceable. The ideal approach is a hybrid model where AI complements human guidance.

The Future of AI in Lifelong Learning and Career Growth

The future of AI in professional development looks promising, with several exciting trends emerging:

1. **AI-Driven Learning Assistants:** Personal AI mentors will guide professionals through their

lifelong learning journey, helping them stay updated with relevant skills.

2. **AI and Augmented Reality (AR) for Hands-On Training:** AR combined with AI will revolutionize vocational training by providing immersive learning experiences.

3. **AI-Enabled Career Navigation:** Future AI systems will offer real-time career coaching, helping professionals navigate complex career transitions with precision.

AI is reshaping lifelong learning and career growth by providing personalized education, optimizing skill development, and offering data-driven career guidance. While challenges exist, AI's role in professional development is invaluable. By embracing AI-powered learning tools, individuals and businesses can stay ahead in an ever-changing job market. The future belongs to those who continuously learn, adapt, and leverage AI as a partner in their career journey.

Chapter 30. The Challenges and Ethical Issues of AI in Education

Artificial intelligence (AI) is transforming education by personalizing learning, automating administrative tasks, and enhancing student engagement. However, the integration of AI in education also brings significant challenges and ethical concerns. Issues such as data privacy, algorithmic bias, digital divide, and the role of human educators in an AI-driven environment must be addressed to ensure AI benefits all learners equitably. This chapter explores the critical challenges and ethical dilemmas surrounding AI in education.

Data Privacy and Security Concerns

AI-powered educational tools collect vast amounts of student data, including learning behaviors, personal information, and performance records. While this data is essential for personalized learning, it raises significant privacy concerns.

1. **Data Ownership and Consent:** Who owns the data collected by AI systems? Should students and parents have full control over how their data is used? Many educational institutions rely on third-party AI platforms, leading to potential misuse of personal information.
2. **Cybersecurity Risks:** AI systems in education are vulnerable to cyberattacks, which can compromise sensitive student records. Schools and universities must invest in robust cybersecurity measures to protect against data breaches.
3. **Informed Consent and Transparency:** Educational institutions must ensure students and parents are aware of what data is being

collected and how it is being used. Transparency is key to building trust in AI-driven education.

Algorithmic Bias and Fairness

AI algorithms are trained on existing data, which can introduce biases that affect student assessments, recommendations, and learning outcomes.

1. **Bias in AI-Based Grading:** AI-driven grading systems can sometimes favor certain demographic groups over others. If trained on biased historical data, these systems may reinforce existing educational inequalities.
2. **Unequal Access to Opportunities:** AI-driven recommendation systems may unintentionally limit students' career or subject choices based on incomplete data, preventing them from exploring diverse learning paths.
3. **Addressing Bias in AI Training Data:** Developers must ensure that AI models are trained on diverse datasets that reflect the needs and backgrounds of all students, avoiding discrimination based on gender, race, or socioeconomic status.

The Digital Divide: Unequal Access to AI in Education

While AI has the potential to enhance learning, it can also widen the gap between students with access to advanced technology and those without.

1. **Lack of Infrastructure in Underprivileged Schools:** Many schools in developing regions lack the necessary infrastructure, such as high-speed internet and modern devices, to support AI-powered learning.
2. **Financial Barriers:** AI-driven education tools, including personalized learning platforms and virtual tutors, often come at a cost that many students and schools cannot afford.
3. **Bridging the Gap:** Governments and educational institutions must work together to ensure equal access to AI tools by investing in digital infrastructure and providing subsidized learning solutions.

The Role of Human Educators in an AI-Driven Classroom

As AI takes over certain aspects of teaching, such as grading and personalized tutoring, there is concern that it may reduce the importance of human teachers. However, the role of educators remains crucial.

1. **AI as a Tool, not a Replacement:** AI can assist teachers by handling administrative tasks, but it cannot replace the human touch in education—such as mentorship, emotional support, and critical thinking development.
2. **Teacher Training for AI Integration:** Educators need proper training to effectively incorporate AI tools into their teaching methods rather than being replaced by them.
3. **Maintaining Human Interaction in Learning:** While AI can provide personalized content, human interaction remains essential for fostering creativity, collaboration, and moral development among students.

Ethical Concerns in AI-Powered Student Monitoring

AI is increasingly being used to monitor students' behavior and performance, raising concerns about surveillance and ethical boundaries.

1. **AI in Exam Proctoring:** Many universities use AI-powered proctoring software to monitor students during online exams. However, these systems have faced criticism for invading

student privacy and falsely flagging innocent behavior as cheating.

2. **Behavioral Analysis and Predictive AI:** Some AI systems track students' facial expressions, attention span, and engagement levels. While this can help improve learning, it raises ethical concerns about constant surveillance and its impact on student well-being.

3. **Balancing Monitoring with Privacy Rights:** Educational institutions must find a balance between using AI for academic integrity and respecting students' privacy and autonomy.

Ethical AI Development and Accountability

To ensure AI benefits all students fairly, ethical guidelines and accountability measures must be put in place.

1. **Transparency in AI Decision-Making:** AI systems should provide explanations for their recommendations and assessments, ensuring students and teachers understand how decisions are made.

2. **Regulatory Frameworks for AI in Education:** Governments and education policymakers must create regulations that govern the ethical use of AI in schools and universities.

3. **Human Oversight of AI Systems:** AI should
   always operate under human supervision to
   ensure it aligns with ethical standards and
   educational goals.

While AI has the potential to revolutionize education, its
implementation must be approached with caution to
address critical challenges and ethical concerns.
Issues such as data privacy, algorithmic bias, unequal
access, and the role of human teachers must be
carefully managed to ensure AI serves as a tool for
positive educational transformation. By prioritizing
ethical AI development, transparency, and equal
access, we can create an AI-enhanced education
system that benefits all learners while maintaining the
human essence of teaching and learning.

SECTION 7: AI in Ethics, Society, and Governance

Chapter 31. The Ethical Boundaries of AI Development

Introduction

Artificial Intelligence (AI) is reshaping industries,
societies, and the way we interact with technology.
However, as AI becomes more integrated into our daily

lives, the ethical concerns surrounding its development grow. Issues such as data privacy, algorithmic bias, accountability, and the potential for AI to surpass human control have led to important debates about setting ethical boundaries in AI development. The challenge lies in ensuring that AI serves humanity responsibly without causing unintended harm or reinforcing societal inequalities.

The Importance of Ethical AI Development

Ethics in AI is not just about preventing harm; it is about ensuring fairness, transparency, and accountability. AI systems influence decisions in healthcare, finance, law enforcement, hiring, and more. Without ethical considerations, these systems can amplify biases, infringe on privacy, or make decisions that lack human empathy.

Developers, policymakers, and businesses must work together to establish guidelines that ensure AI is developed responsibly. Ethical AI should respect human rights, uphold transparency, and promote inclusivity while minimizing risks associated with misuse and unintended consequences.

Bias in AI: The Challenge of Fairness

One of the biggest ethical concerns in AI development is algorithmic bias. AI systems learn from historical data, and if this data is biased, the AI can make discriminatory decisions.

1. **Racial and Gender Bias:** AI-powered hiring systems have been found to favor certain demographics while disadvantaging others due to biased training data. Similarly, facial recognition technology has been criticized for misidentifying individuals from minority groups.
2. **Bias in Law Enforcement:** AI-driven predictive policing has raised concerns as it can reinforce racial profiling, leading to unfair treatment of certain communities.
3. **Ensuring Fair AI:** Developers must implement bias detection and mitigation techniques to ensure that AI decisions are equitable. This includes using diverse training data and regularly auditing AI systems for biased outcomes.

Privacy Concerns and Data Protection

AI relies heavily on data, but collecting and analyzing large amounts of personal information raises serious privacy issues.

1. **Mass Surveillance:** Governments and corporations use AI to monitor individuals, often without consent. Facial recognition and behavioral tracking tools can invade personal privacy, leading to ethical concerns about surveillance.
2. **Data Ownership:** Many AI systems rely on user-generated data, but who owns this data? Companies frequently collect, store, and analyze personal information without providing users with full control over how their data is used.
3. **Regulating Data Use:** Strict data protection laws, such as the General Data Protection Regulation (GDPR) in Europe, set an example for ethical AI development. Organizations must prioritize transparency and allow individuals to control how their data is collected and used.

Accountability and Transparency in AI Decision-Making

AI systems make decisions that impact human lives, from approving loans to diagnosing medical conditions. However, AI models often operate as "black boxes," meaning their decision-making processes are not easily understood.

1. **The Problem of Black-Box AI:** Many AI models, especially deep learning systems, lack transparency, making it difficult to explain how they arrive at decisions.
2. **Who is Responsible for AI Mistakes?** If an AI-driven self-driving car causes an accident, who is responsible—the developer, the manufacturer, or the user? Clear accountability structures must be established to prevent ethical dilemmas.
3. **Explainable AI:** Researchers are developing AI models that provide clear explanations for their decisions. This is crucial for ensuring accountability, especially in high-stakes fields like healthcare and criminal justice.

The Risk of AI Replacing Human Jobs

While AI has the potential to enhance productivity, there is growing concern that it could replace human workers, leading to mass unemployment and economic instability.

1. **Automation in Industries:** AI is already replacing jobs in manufacturing, customer service, and even creative fields like journalism and music composition.
2. **The Need for Reskilling:** Ethical AI development must include policies that support workers

through retraining programs, ensuring they can transition into new roles rather than being left behind.

3. **AI as an Assistant, not a Replacement:** AI should be designed to augment human capabilities rather than entirely replace human workers. The focus should be on collaboration between humans and AI.

The Threat of Autonomous AI and Lack of Human Control

One of the biggest ethical fears surrounding AI is the development of autonomous systems that act without human intervention.

1. **Military AI and Lethal Autonomous Weapons:** The use of AI in warfare raises serious ethical questions. Should machines have the power to decide who lives and dies? Many experts call for a ban on AI-driven weapons to prevent uncontrollable conflicts.

2. **Superintelligent AI Risks:** If AI surpasses human intelligence, it could become difficult to control. While this remains a theoretical concern, researchers argue that AI must always remain aligned with human values.

3. **The Importance of Human Oversight:** AI should never operate without human supervision in

critical decision-making areas. Ethical AI must always have a "human-in-the-loop" approach to prevent unintended consequences.

Regulations and Ethical AI Development Frameworks

To ensure AI is developed responsibly, international cooperation is necessary to establish legal and ethical frameworks.

1. **Global AI Ethics Standards:** Organizations such as UNESCO, the European Union, and AI ethics committees worldwide are working on policies to regulate AI.
2. **Corporate Responsibility:** Companies developing AI systems must follow ethical guidelines, ensuring their technology does not harm individuals or society.
3. **Public Awareness and AI Literacy:** People must be educated about AI's capabilities and risks so they can make informed decisions about how AI should be used in their lives.

AI has the potential to transform the world for the better, but without ethical boundaries, it could lead to unintended harm. Developers, policymakers, and society must work together to ensure AI remains fair, transparent, and accountable. Setting ethical boundaries in AI development is not just a technical challenge—it is a moral responsibility. By prioritizing human rights, fairness, and responsible innovation, we can create AI systems that truly benefit humanity while minimizing risks.

Chapter 32. AI and the Future of Employment: Friend or Foe?

Artificial Intelligence (AI) is revolutionizing industries at an unprecedented pace, automating tasks, improving efficiency, and reshaping the global workforce. While some see AI as a tool that enhances human productivity, others fear it will lead to widespread job displacement. Will AI be a friend that creates new opportunities, or a foe that replaces human workers? The answer lies in how societies adapt to these technological advancements and implement policies that ensure a balanced and ethical integration of AI into the workforce.

The Fear of Job Loss: Is AI Replacing Humans?

The most common fear associated with AI is that it will eliminate jobs, particularly in sectors that rely on repetitive tasks. Automation is already replacing human labor in industries such as manufacturing, customer service, logistics, and even creative fields like journalism and music composition.

1. **Manufacturing and Automation:** Factories have increasingly turned to AI-powered robots to assemble products faster and with greater precision than human workers. This has reduced the need for manual labor in assembly lines, leading to concerns about mass unemployment.

2. **Customer Service and AI Chatbots:** AI-driven chatbots and virtual assistants handle customer queries, reducing the need for human call center employees. While this improves efficiency, it also threatens jobs in customer support.

3. **AI in Creative Fields:** AI can now write news articles, generate music, and even create artwork. This raises concerns about whether human writers, musicians, and artists will become obsolete.

While AI is indeed automating many jobs, history suggests that technological advancements often create new types of employment rather than leading to permanent job losses. The challenge is ensuring that workers are prepared for these new roles.

The Jobs AI is Creating: New Opportunities in the AI Era

While AI is replacing some jobs, it is also generating new employment opportunities in emerging fields. These include roles that require managing, programming, and working alongside AI systems.

1. **AI and Data Science Jobs:** The rise of AI has created high demand for AI specialists, machine learning engineers, and data scientists who develop and maintain AI systems.
2. **Human-AI Collaboration Roles:** New job roles involve working alongside AI, such as AI-assisted healthcare professionals, financial analysts using AI-driven insights, and educators integrating AI into classrooms.
3. **Ethics and AI Governance Jobs:** As AI raises ethical concerns, there is a growing need for AI ethicists, policy makers, and compliance officers who can ensure AI systems are used responsibly.
4. **New Industries Fueled by AI:** AI-driven advancements in space exploration, biotechnology, and green energy are creating new industries, leading to job opportunities that did not exist a decade ago.

While AI is transforming the nature of work, the real challenge is ensuring workers can transition into these emerging fields through reskilling and education.

The Need for Reskilling and Adaptation

To ensure AI remains a friend rather than a foe in the job market, reskilling and continuous learning must become a priority. Governments, businesses, and educational institutions must collaborate to provide workers with the skills needed to thrive in an AI-driven world.

1. **Lifelong Learning:** Workers must embrace continuous education to keep up with evolving AI technologies. Online courses, certifications, and vocational training can help bridge the skills gap.
2. **Corporate Training Programs:** Companies should invest in training programs that help employees transition into new AI-assisted roles rather than simply replacing them.
3. **Government Policies for Workforce Development:** Governments must implement policies that support reskilling initiatives, ensuring that workers are not left behind as industries evolve.

By focusing on education and adaptability, societies can transform AI into a tool that empowers workers rather than displacing them.

AI as an Assistant, not a Replacement

The best approach to integrating AI into the workforce is to use it as an assistant rather than a replacement for human intelligence. AI can handle repetitive and time-consuming tasks, allowing humans to focus on creativity, problem-solving, and interpersonal interactions.

1. **AI in Healthcare:** AI-powered diagnostic tools assist doctors in detecting diseases more accurately, but they do not replace the need for human doctors who provide empathy and decision-making.
2. **AI in Business:** AI-driven analytics help businesses make informed decisions, but human leaders are still needed to interpret results and develop strategic plans.
3. **AI in Education:** AI can personalize learning experiences, but teachers remain essential for mentoring, critical thinking development, and emotional support.

When AI is designed to complement human skills rather than replace them, it becomes a powerful ally in the workplace.

The Future of Work: Balancing AI and Human Roles

The future of employment will not be defined by AI replacing humans, but rather by how well societies adapt to the AI revolution. Companies that prioritize human-AI collaboration will thrive, while workers who continuously adapt and learn new skills will find new opportunities.

Governments, businesses, and workers must work together to ensure AI serves as a friend rather than a foe. By investing in education, ethical AI development, and policies that support workforce adaptation, we can create a future where AI enhances human potential rather than diminishing it.

AI is not the end of work—it is the beginning of a new era of human-AI collaboration. Whether AI becomes a friend or a foe depends on how we choose to integrate it into our societies and workplaces.

Chapter 33. AI in Law, Justice, and Governance

Artificial Intelligence (AI) is rapidly transforming various sectors, and the legal system is no exception. From automating legal research to assisting in judicial decision-making, AI is reshaping how law, justice, and governance function. However, this transformation brings both opportunities and challenges. While AI can improve efficiency, reduce bias, and enhance decision-making, it also raises ethical concerns, particularly regarding accountability and fairness. The key question remains: Can AI be a reliable partner in law and governance without compromising justice and human rights?

AI in Legal Research and Case Analysis

One of the most time-consuming aspects of legal practice is researching case laws, statutes, and precedents. AI-powered legal research tools have revolutionized this process by quickly analyzing vast amounts of legal data and providing relevant insights.

1. **Automated Case Law Analysis:** AI algorithms can scan thousands of past legal cases, identify relevant precedents, and suggest applicable laws within seconds—something that would take human lawyers' weeks to accomplish.
2. **Legal Document Automation:** AI tools assist in drafting contracts, agreements, and legal documents, ensuring consistency and accuracy while saving lawyer's valuable time.
3. **Predictive Legal Analytics:** AI-powered systems analyze previous judgments to predict the likely outcome of a case based on historical data, helping lawyers formulate stronger legal strategies.

By streamlining legal research, AI allows lawyers to focus on higher-level tasks such as argumentation, negotiation, and client advocacy.

AI in the Courtroom: Can AI Assist Judges?

Judicial decision-making requires careful analysis of laws, evidence, and ethical considerations. While AI is not meant to replace human judges, it can play a significant role in supporting judicial processes.

1. **AI-Powered Case Prioritization:** AI can help courts prioritize cases based on complexity, urgency, and legal precedent, ensuring a fairer and more efficient judicial system.
2. **Sentencing and Risk Assessment:** Some legal systems use AI to assess the likelihood of reoffending when determining bail or sentencing, helping judges make informed decisions. However, concerns remain about potential biases in AI models.
3. **AI as a Judicial Assistant:** AI tools can help judges summarize lengthy case files, highlight relevant arguments, and detect inconsistencies, enabling more informed decision-making.

While AI can enhance judicial efficiency, it must be used cautiously to prevent over-reliance on technology in making final legal determinations.

AI in Governance and Public Administration

AI has the potential to transform governance by making public administration more efficient, transparent, and data-driven. Governments worldwide are integrating AI into policymaking, law enforcement, and citizen services.

1. **Smart Policymaking:** AI-driven data analysis helps governments assess social and economic trends, enabling informed policy decisions in areas such as healthcare, education, and climate change.
2. **Fraud Detection and Anti-Corruption Measures:** AI systems can analyze financial transactions, detect anomalies, and identify corruption patterns, helping governments combat fraud.
3. **AI-Powered Public Services:** Many governments use AI chatbots and virtual assistants to improve public service delivery, making it easier for citizens to access information on taxes, benefits, and legal procedures.

By enhancing governance efficiency, AI can improve citizens' trust in government institutions and streamline bureaucratic processes.

AI in Law Enforcement: Enhancing Justice or Invading Privacy?

Law enforcement agencies increasingly use AI for crime prevention, investigation, and surveillance. While AI can improve public safety, it also raises concerns about privacy and ethical implications.

1. **Facial Recognition and Crime Detection:** AI-powered facial recognition technology helps law enforcement track criminals, but its misuse can lead to privacy violations and wrongful arrests.
2. **Predictive Policing:** AI algorithms analyze crime patterns and predict where crimes are likely to occur, enabling proactive policing. However, if trained on biased data, such systems risk reinforcing discrimination.
3. **Digital Evidence Analysis:** AI can process vast amounts of digital evidence from surveillance footage, social media, and phone records, aiding criminal investigations.

Governments must balance AI's role in law enforcement with ethical guidelines to ensure fairness and protect civil liberties.

Challenges and Ethical Concerns of AI in Law and Governance

While AI offers numerous benefits in the legal and governance sectors, it also presents challenges that must be carefully addressed.

1. **Algorithmic Bias:** AI systems trained on biased legal data may reinforce existing prejudices, leading to unfair sentencing and discriminatory policing.
2. **Lack of Transparency:** AI decision-making processes are often opaque, making it difficult to challenge or appeal decisions influenced by AI.
3. **Accountability and Legal Responsibility:** Who is responsible when an AI system makes a mistake? The lack of clear legal frameworks for AI accountability remains a critical issue.
4. **Privacy and Surveillance Risks:** The use of AI for mass surveillance raises concerns about human rights violations and government overreach.

Governments and legal institutions must develop clear guidelines to ensure AI in law and governance is used ethically and responsibly.

The Future of AI in Law and Governance

As AI continues to evolve, its role in law, justice, and governance will only expand. However, its integration must be guided by human oversight, ethical considerations, and legal safeguards.

1. **Regulating AI in Law:** Governments must implement AI-specific legal frameworks to prevent misuse and ensure AI serves justice rather than undermining it.
2. **Human-AI Collaboration:** AI should act as an assistant to legal professionals, not as a replacement for human judgment and ethical reasoning.
3. **Transparency and Explainability:** AI models used in legal and governance systems must be transparent, allowing for human review and accountability.

The ultimate goal should be to create an AI-powered legal and governance system that enhances human capabilities while upholding justice, fairness, and ethical integrity. AI, when used correctly, can become a valuable partner in ensuring a more efficient and equitable legal system.

Chapter 34. AI and Bias: The Human Factor Behind Machine Decisions

Artificial Intelligence (AI) is often perceived as objective and impartial, free from the biases that influence human decision-making. However, AI systems are not inherently neutral. They are created, trained, and fine-tuned by humans, which means they can inherit human biases—sometimes amplifying them in unexpected ways. Bias in AI can have significant consequences, affecting everything from hiring decisions to criminal sentencing, healthcare diagnoses, and financial lending. Understanding how and why AI systems develop biases is crucial to ensuring fair, ethical, and responsible AI deployment.

What Is AI Bias?

AI bias refers to systematic errors in AI systems that lead to unfair, prejudiced, or discriminatory outcomes. These biases stem from the data AI models is trained on, the algorithms used, and even the decisions made by AI developers. Bias in AI can manifest in various ways, including racial, gender, socioeconomic, and cultural biases.

For example, an AI-driven hiring tool trained on past job applicant data may favor male candidates over female candidates if historical hiring patterns were biased. Similarly, facial recognition systems have been found to misidentify individuals with darker skin tones more frequently than those with lighter skin tones, demonstrating racial bias.

How Does AI Bias Occur?

1. **Bias in Training Data**

2. AI systems learn from historical data. If this data contains biases, the AI will absorb and replicate them. For example, if past criminal sentencing data shows racial disparities, an AI-powered legal prediction tool may perpetuate those disparities.

3. **Algorithmic Bias**

The mathematical models used in AI decision-making can introduce bias. Some algorithms weigh certain variables more heavily than others, leading to skewed results. Even slight imbalances in algorithmic design can result in discrimination.

4. **Human Bias in AI Development**

AI systems reflect the perspectives of their developers. If AI engineers unconsciously introduce their own biases into model training and design, these biases become embedded in the system. Decisions about which data to include, how to structure models, and what goals to prioritize all shape AI outcomes.

5. Feedback Loop Bias

AI models are often trained on past decisions, which means they can reinforce existing societal biases. For instance, if a predictive policing AI is trained on historical crime data that over-polices certain communities, it may continue to disproportionately target those areas, reinforcing bias rather than eliminating it.

6. Selection Bias

AI models may be trained on non-representative datasets that exclude certain demographics, leading to biased outputs. If an AI medical diagnosis system is trained primarily on data from young, healthy individuals, it may fail to provide accurate diagnoses for older or more diverse populations.

Real-World Consequences of AI Bias

1. Hiring Discrimination

AI-driven hiring systems have been shown to favor male applicants over female candidates due to biases in past hiring data. This can reinforce gender inequality in the workplace.

2. **Racial Bias in Law Enforcement**

AI-powered facial recognition systems have disproportionately misidentified people of color, leading to wrongful arrests and violations of civil rights.

3. **Healthcare Disparities**

AI in medicine may provide less accurate diagnoses for underrepresented populations if its training data lacks diversity. Some AI-driven health risk assessments have been found to underestimate the health risks of Black patients compared to white patients.

4. **Financial Inequality**

AI-driven credit scoring and loan approval systems may disadvantage minority groups if they are trained on historical data reflecting discriminatory lending practices.

5. **Misinformation and Media Bias**

AI-powered news recommendation systems may create echo chambers by reinforcing biased viewpoints, leading to polarization and misinformation.

Can AI Be Made Bias-Free?

Completely eliminating bias from AI is challenging, but several strategies can help minimize it:

1. **Diverse and Inclusive Training Data**

Ensuring AI models are trained on data that accurately represents different demographics, cultures, and perspectives helps reduce bias.

2. **Bias Detection and Auditing**

Regularly testing AI models for bias and conducting audits can identify and correct unintended discriminatory patterns. Independent AI ethics committees can help ensure transparency.

3. **Explainable AI (XAI)**

AI models should be designed to provide clear explanations for their decisions, making it easier to identify and correct biases.

4. **Human Oversight and Intervention**

AI should be used as a tool to assist, not replace, human decision-making. Human oversight is essential to catch and correct biased AI outputs.

5. **Regulatory and Ethical Frameworks**

Governments and organizations must implement ethical guidelines and legal regulations to prevent biased AI from harming marginalized communities.

The Future of AI and Bias Mitigation

As AI continues to play a growing role in society, ensuring fairness and reducing bias will be an ongoing challenge. Researchers and policymakers must work together to create AI systems that enhance human decision-making without reinforcing existing prejudices. By promoting diversity in AI development, implementing bias-detection measures, and prioritizing ethical considerations, we can build AI that serves all of humanity fairly and equitably.

AI is not inherently biased—the human factor behind AI decisions determines whether it will be a force for fairness or inequality. The responsibility lies with developers, businesses, and governments to ensure AI technology is used ethically and responsibly.

Chapter 35. The Role of Governments in Regulating AI

Artificial Intelligence (AI) is transforming industries, economies, and societies at an unprecedented pace. While AI presents immense opportunities for innovation, efficiency, and economic growth, it also raises concerns about privacy, security, bias, and ethical use. The rapid advancement of AI technologies has outpaced existing regulatory frameworks, creating a pressing need for governments to establish guidelines that ensure responsible AI development and deployment.

Governments worldwide are now faced with the challenge of balancing innovation with regulation—creating policies that encourage AI growth while protecting citizens from potential risks. This chapter explores the crucial role of governments in regulating AI, the challenges involved, and the strategies being implemented to create a fair, safe, and ethical AI-driven world.

Why AI Regulation Is Necessary

The regulation of AI is essential to address several key concerns:

1. **Ethical AI Development and Use**

2. AI systems must be designed and deployed with ethical considerations in mind. Without proper oversight, AI can be misused for mass surveillance, misinformation campaigns, and autonomous weapons development. Governments must ensure that AI aligns with human values and rights.

3. **Bias and Discrimination**

AI can inherit and amplify human biases, leading to unfair treatment in hiring, lending, healthcare, and law enforcement. Regulations can mandate fairness, accountability, and transparency in AI decision-making to prevent discrimination.

4. Privacy Protection

AI-powered surveillance, facial recognition, and data analytics can infringe on personal privacy. Governments must enforce strict data protection laws to prevent misuse of sensitive information.

5. Economic Disruptions and Job Losses

AI-driven automation threatens traditional job markets, leading to economic displacement. Policies are needed to support reskilling programs, universal basic income (UBI), or other measures to assist displaced workers.

6. AI Safety and Security

AI systems can be vulnerable to hacking, misinformation, and malicious use. Governments must establish cybersecurity protocols to safeguard AI applications in critical sectors like defense, finance, and healthcare.

7. Accountability and Liability

When AI systems make mistakes—such as wrongful arrests due to biased facial recognition or incorrect medical diagnoses—determining liability becomes difficult. Regulatory frameworks must define legal responsibilities for AI developers, companies, and users.

Challenges in AI Regulation

Despite the urgent need for AI regulations, governments face several challenges in designing and enforcing them:

1. The Rapid Evolution of AI

AI technology is advancing so quickly that regulations risk becoming outdated before they are even implemented. Policymakers struggle to keep up with new AI capabilities.

2. Global Disparities in AI Governance

Different countries have different approaches to AI regulation. While the European Union (EU) has taken a strict stance with the AI Act, other regions, such as the U.S. and China, have varying levels of oversight, making international cooperation difficult.

3. Balancing Innovation and Regulation

Overregulation may stifle innovation and deter AI research and investment, while under-regulation could lead to harmful consequences. Governments must strike a balance between encouraging progress and ensuring safety.

4. Lack of Public Awareness and Understanding

Many policymakers and citizens lack technical knowledge about AI, making it challenging to craft effective and informed regulations.

5. Jurisdiction and Cross-Border AI Issues

AI systems operate across borders, creating complications in regulation enforcement. An AI model trained in one country can be deployed globally, making it difficult to impose national laws on international AI usage.

Global Approaches to AI Regulation

The European Union (EU): The AI Act

The EU has taken a proactive approach to AI regulation by proposing the **AI Act**, the world's first comprehensive legal framework for AI. The AI Act categorizes AI systems based on risk levels:

- **Unacceptable Risk AI** (banned) – AI used for mass surveillance, social scoring, or manipulative practices.

- **High-Risk AI** (strictly regulated) – AI used in healthcare, law enforcement, finance, and hiring.
- **Limited Risk AI** (transparency requirements) – AI that generates deepfakes or chatbots.
- **Minimal Risk AI** (no major restrictions) – AI applications like recommendation algorithms.

This framework aims to ensure AI safety while allowing low-risk AI applications to thrive with minimal regulation.

United States: A Sector-Specific Approach

The U.S. has adopted a decentralized, industry-specific approach to AI regulation rather than a single national framework. Key efforts include:

- The **White House AI Bill of Rights**, which outlines principles for safe and ethical AI use.
- **NIST AI Risk Management Framework**, which provides voluntary guidelines for AI developers.
- Various state-level laws on AI applications in hiring, facial recognition, and data privacy.

The U.S. approach prioritizes innovation but lacks uniform federal oversight, leading to fragmented AI governance.

China: Strict AI Control

China has implemented some of the world's strictest AI regulations, focusing on government control, censorship, and national security. Regulations include:

- Laws requiring AI-generated content to be labeled as such.
- Restrictions on deepfake technology and misinformation.
- Strict control over AI applications in media, finance, and social platforms.

China's AI regulations emphasize state power, limiting the influence of foreign tech companies while fostering domestic AI growth.

Other Countries

- **Canada**: The **Artificial Intelligence and Data Act (AIDA)** seeks to regulate high-risk AI and ensure responsible AI adoption.
- **United Kingdom**: The UK follows a **light-touch approach**, allowing AI development with minimal restrictions while monitoring risks.
- **India**: India is developing a framework that balances AI innovation with ethical guidelines.

Key Strategies for Effective AI Regulation

1. International Cooperation

Since AI is a global technology, nations must collaborate on international regulatory standards, just as they do with cybersecurity and climate change policies. Organizations like the United Nations (UN) and the Organization for Economic Co-operation and Development (OECD) play a key role in global AI governance.

2. Ethical AI Guidelines

Governments should establish AI ethics boards to oversee responsible AI development. These guidelines should promote fairness, transparency, accountability, and human oversight.

3. Public and Private Sector Collaboration

Governments should work alongside AI companies, academic researchers, and civil society to create balanced policies that encourage innovation while mitigating risks.

4. Transparency and Explainability Requirements

AI systems should be required to provide explainable decision-making processes, especially in high-stakes fields like healthcare, criminal justice, and finance.

5. Stronger Consumer Protection Laws

AI should not be allowed to exploit consumers through deceptive practices, unfair pricing, or biased algorithms. Strengthening consumer rights is essential.

6. Continuous AI Monitoring and Adaptability

AI regulations should be flexible and continuously updated as technology evolves. Regulatory sandboxes—where AI systems can be tested under controlled conditions—can help policymakers understand AI risks before enacting strict laws.

Governments play a crucial role in ensuring that AI is developed and deployed responsibly. Without proper oversight, AI could lead to discrimination, privacy violations, and economic instability. However, overregulation could stifle innovation and technological progress.

The future of AI governance lies in a balanced approach that prioritizes ethics, fairness, and security while allowing businesses and researchers to innovate. As AI continues to evolve, governments must remain proactive, adaptive, and globally cooperative to ensure that AI serves humanity rather than harms it.

SECTION 8: AI in Daily Life and Smart Living

Chapter 36. How AI is Revolutionizing Everyday Life

Artificial Intelligence (AI) has seamlessly integrated into our daily lives, reshaping the way we work, communicate, shop, and even take care of our health. Once a concept limited to science fiction, AI is now a reality that enhances convenience, efficiency, and personalization in countless ways. From voice assistants and smart home devices to medical diagnostics and financial services, AI-driven technologies are transforming modern living. This chapter explores the profound impact of AI on everyday life, highlighting the areas where it has become indispensable.

AI in Communication and Personal Assistance

One of the most noticeable ways AI has changed daily life is through communication. AI-powered virtual assistants like Siri, Google Assistant, and Alexa help users perform tasks with simple voice commands. These assistants can set reminders, provide weather updates, answer questions, and even control smart home devices, making life more convenient.

In messaging and email, AI enhances communication by providing **smart replies**, **predictive text**, and **language translation**. Features like Gmail's Smart Compose and Microsoft's AI-driven grammar checker help users write more efficiently. AI chatbots also assist customers by answering queries instantly on websites and social media, improving customer service experiences.

AI in Smart Homes and Everyday Convenience

Smart home technology has become a key area where AI is revolutionizing daily life. AI-powered home assistants like Google Nest and Amazon Echo allow users to control lighting, temperature, and security systems using voice commands or mobile apps. AI-driven thermostats like **Nest Learning Thermostat** adapt to a person's schedule, optimizing energy use and reducing costs.

AI-powered **robot vacuums**, such as Roomba, use intelligent mapping to clean homes more efficiently. Smart refrigerators track food inventory and suggest recipes based on available ingredients, while AI-enabled security cameras enhance home safety with facial recognition and automated alerts. These technologies simplify household tasks and provide a more comfortable living environment.

AI in Healthcare and Wellness

AI has had a transformative impact on healthcare, improving both accessibility and accuracy. Wearable health devices like **Fitbit** and **Apple Watch** use AI to monitor heart rates, sleep patterns, and physical activity, providing users with insights into their well-being. AI-powered apps analyze symptoms and offer preliminary diagnoses, allowing individuals to make informed decisions about their health.

In hospitals, AI assists doctors with medical imaging analysis, drug discovery, and robotic surgeries. AI systems like IBM Watson can process vast amounts of medical data to recommend personalized treatment plans. Telemedicine platforms powered by AI enable patients to consult with doctors remotely, improving healthcare access, especially in remote areas.

AI in Shopping and Personalized Experiences

Online shopping has been revolutionized by AI, which enhances user experience through personalization. AI algorithms analyze browsing history and preferences to recommend products on platforms like **Amazon**,

Netflix, and **Spotify**. Chatbots provide instant customer support, while AI-driven **visual search** allows users to find products using images instead of keywords.

AI is also transforming in-store shopping. Retailers use AI-powered **smart mirrors** and **virtual try-ons** to help customers visualize clothing, makeup, and accessories before purchasing. AI-enabled checkout systems, such as Amazon's **Just Walk Out** technology, eliminate the need for cashiers, making shopping faster and more convenient.

AI in Transportation and Navigation

AI plays a crucial role in making transportation safer and more efficient. Navigation apps like **Google Maps** and **Waze** use AI to provide real-time traffic updates, optimize routes, and estimate arrival times. AI-powered ride-hailing services like **Uber** and **Lyft** match riders with drivers efficiently, reducing wait times.

Self-driving car technology, developed by companies like Tesla and Waymo, is powered by AI to enhance road safety and reduce human errors. AI systems analyze sensor data to detect pedestrians, traffic signs, and obstacles, allowing autonomous vehicles to navigate roads with increasing precision.

AI in Finance and Banking

AI has significantly improved the way people manage their finances. Banks and financial institutions use AI for **fraud detection**, monitoring transactions for suspicious activity and alerting customers in real time. AI-driven chatbots assist users with banking inquiries, while robo-advisors like **Betterment** and **Wealthfront** provide automated investment advice based on market trends and personal financial goals.

AI also powers **budgeting and expense tracking apps** like Mint, which analyze spending habits and offer financial recommendations. In the stock market, AI-driven trading algorithms analyze vast amounts of data to make high-speed investment decisions, optimizing returns for investors.

AI in Education and Learning

AI is reshaping education by making learning more personalized and accessible. AI-powered platforms like **Duolingo**, **Khan Academy**, and **Coursera** adapt lessons based on a student's progress, helping them learn at their own pace. AI-driven tutoring systems provide instant feedback, making education more interactive and effective.

Voice recognition technology assists students with disabilities, while AI-powered plagiarism detectors ensure academic integrity. AI is also used in admissions and career counseling, helping students make informed choices about their education and future.

AI in Entertainment and Creativity

AI is changing the way we consume entertainment. Streaming platforms like **Netflix**, **Spotify**, and **YouTube** use AI to recommend content based on viewing habits. AI-generated music and art are gaining popularity, with tools like OpenAI's **Jukebox** creating music and **DeepDream** producing unique digital artwork.

In the film industry, AI is used for CGI effects, scriptwriting assistance, and even generating realistic deepfake technology. AI-powered video game engines create more immersive gaming experiences by adapting difficulty levels and storytelling based on player behavior.

Challenges and Ethical Considerations

While AI enhances everyday life in many ways, it also presents challenges. Privacy concerns arise as AI collects and analyzes vast amounts of personal data. AI-driven automation may displace jobs, requiring workers to reskill for new roles. Bias in AI algorithms can lead to unfair outcomes in hiring, healthcare, and law enforcement.

To address these concerns, ethical AI development must prioritize transparency, fairness, and accountability. Governments and companies must work together to establish guidelines that ensure AI serves society responsibly and equitably.

AI has become an essential part of modern life, transforming how we communicate, shop, travel, learn, and receive healthcare. As AI technology continues to advance, it will further enhance convenience, efficiency, and personalization in daily activities. However, responsible AI development and regulation are crucial to ensure its benefits are distributed fairly and ethically.

The future of AI promises even more innovation, making everyday life smarter, safer, and more connected. As AI continues to evolve, it will redefine what is possible, improving the quality of life for people around the world.

Chapter 37. AI and Human Well-Being: The Role of Smart Assistants

Artificial Intelligence (AI) has become an integral part of our daily lives, contributing significantly to human well-being through the use of smart assistants. These AI-powered tools are designed to make life easier, healthier, and more productive. From voice-activated virtual assistants like Siri, Alexa, and Google Assistant to AI-powered health monitors and mental wellness apps, smart assistants are helping individuals manage their routines, enhance productivity, and improve overall well-being.

Enhancing Daily Productivity and Convenience

One of the primary roles of AI-powered smart assistants is to simplify everyday tasks. Voice assistants can set reminders, schedule appointments, send messages, and provide real-time information, reducing the mental burden of daily responsibilities. Smart assistants can also automate household tasks, controlling smart home devices like lighting, thermostats, and security systems with simple voice commands or app-based controls.

In professional settings, AI-driven virtual assistants help manage emails, organize meetings, and provide timely notifications, allowing users to focus on more important tasks. By automating routine activities, smart assistants free up time and mental space, leading to increased efficiency and reduced stress.

AI in Health and Wellness Monitoring

AI-powered smart assistants play a vital role in promoting health and well-being by helping individuals track their physical and mental health. Wearable devices like the Apple Watch and Fitbit use AI to monitor heart rate, sleep patterns, and activity levels, providing real-time health insights. These devices encourage users to adopt healthier lifestyles by sending reminders to move, hydrate, or practice mindfulness.

AI-driven health apps can analyze symptoms, suggest possible causes, and even recommend whether medical attention is needed. Virtual health assistants like Ada and Babylon Health provide preliminary medical assessments based on AI algorithms, helping users make informed health decisions. Additionally, AI-powered smart assistants can remind individuals to take their medications on time, ensuring better adherence to treatment plans.

Supporting Mental Health and Emotional Well-Being

Smart assistants are not only improving physical health but also playing a crucial role in mental well-being. AI-powered mental health chatbots like Woebot and Wysa offer conversational support, helping users manage stress, anxiety, and depression. These assistants use natural language processing (NLP) to provide therapeutic guidance, mindfulness exercises, and cognitive behavioral therapy (CBT) techniques, making mental health support more accessible.

Meditation and relaxation apps such as Headspace and Calm integrate AI to personalize mindfulness sessions, adapting to the user's mood and preferences. Smart assistants can also help create a more calming environment by playing soothing music, adjusting lighting, or suggesting relaxation exercises.

Smart Assistants for Personalized Learning and Skill Development

AI-driven smart assistants contribute to lifelong learning and skill development by providing personalized learning experiences. Language-learning platforms like Duolingo use AI to adapt lessons to the user's progress, while AI tutors like ScribeSense provide real-time feedback on writing and comprehension.

Smart assistants can also help individuals develop new skills by recommending online courses, offering step-by-step instructions for various tasks, and even assisting in creative projects. Whether learning a new language, improving time management, or mastering a musical instrument, AI-powered tools provide tailored support for continuous growth.

Encouraging Work-Life Balance and Stress Reduction

With increasing demands in both professional and personal life, maintaining a work-life balance has become a challenge. Smart assistants help by managing schedules, setting boundaries, and promoting self-care. AI-driven time management tools analyze work habits and suggest improvements to optimize productivity while minimizing burnout.

Some AI-powered assistants can automatically schedule breaks, remind users to take deep breaths, and suggest moments of relaxation throughout the day. They also encourage mindful screen usage by setting screen time limits and offering digital detox recommendations. By helping individuals balance work and leisure, smart assistants contribute to overall well-being and happiness.

AI in Safety and Security for Peace of Mind

Smart assistants are also enhancing safety and security, providing peace of mind to users. AI-powered security systems can detect unusual activities, send real-time alerts, and even recognize familiar faces through facial recognition technology. Voice-activated emergency response features allow users to call for help instantly, making smart assistants valuable in crisis situations.

For elderly individuals or those with disabilities, AI-powered assistants can offer additional support by detecting falls, providing medication reminders, and enabling hands-free communication with caregivers. These features ensure that vulnerable individuals receive timely assistance, promoting a safer living environment.

Ethical Considerations and Privacy Concerns

Despite the numerous benefits of AI-powered smart assistants, there are ethical concerns regarding data privacy and security. Smart assistants continuously process personal data to enhance their functionality, raising concerns about unauthorized access, data breaches, and misuse of personal information.

To address these concerns, tech companies are implementing stronger data protection measures, giving users more control over their information. Transparency in AI decision-making and responsible AI development are crucial to ensuring that smart assistants continue to serve human well-being without compromising privacy.

AI-powered smart assistants have become indispensable in modern life, improving productivity, health, mental well-being, education, and security. By automating routine tasks, providing personalized support, and enhancing overall convenience, these tools empower individuals to lead healthier, more balanced lives.

As AI continues to evolve, smart assistants will become even more sophisticated, offering deeper insights and more intuitive interactions. However, ensuring ethical AI development and responsible usage will be essential in maintaining trust and maximizing the benefits of AI for human well-being.

Chapter 38. AI in Smart Homes and IoT

The integration of Artificial Intelligence (AI) with the Internet of Things (IoT) has transformed modern homes into highly efficient, intelligent living spaces. AI-powered smart homes offer convenience, security, energy efficiency, and enhanced automation, making everyday life more comfortable and sustainable. As AI continues to evolve, its role in smart homes is expanding, allowing for personalized experiences, real-time decision-making, and seamless connectivity between devices.

The Foundation of AI in Smart Homes

AI-driven smart homes operate through a network of interconnected IoT devices that communicate with each other, learning from user behavior to optimize home automation. Smart assistants such as Amazon Alexa, Google Assistant, and Apple's Siri act as central hubs, controlling various devices via voice commands or mobile applications. These AI-powered systems analyze data from sensors, cameras, and appliances to anticipate user needs and automate tasks, reducing the need for manual input.

Smart Home Automation: Enhancing Convenience

One of the key benefits of AI in smart homes is automation, which simplifies routine tasks and enhances convenience. AI-driven systems can adjust lighting, temperature, and security settings based on user preferences and real-time environmental data.

For example, smart thermostats like Nest and Ecobee learn household routines and adjust temperatures automatically to optimize comfort and energy efficiency. AI-powered lighting systems can turn lights on and off based on motion detection, voice commands, or preset schedules. Smart kitchen appliances, such as AI-enabled refrigerators and ovens, can suggest recipes, track food expiration dates, and even order groceries when supplies are running low.

By automating daily functions, AI in smart homes reduces the cognitive load on residents, allowing them to focus on more important tasks while enjoying a seamless living experience.

AI-Driven Security and Surveillance

Security is a top priority for smart homes, and AI has significantly enhanced home surveillance and safety measures. AI-powered security cameras, such as Ring and Nest Cam, use facial recognition and motion detection to identify authorized individuals and detect suspicious activity. These systems send real-time alerts to homeowners, allowing them to monitor their property remotely.

Smart doorbells with AI-driven video analytics provide two-way communication, enabling users to interact with visitors from anywhere. AI-powered alarm systems can distinguish between routine movements and potential security threats, reducing false alarms and improving response times. Additionally, AI-integrated smart locks can grant or restrict access to individuals based on voice recognition or mobile app controls, ensuring enhanced security for residents.

Energy Efficiency and Sustainability

AI plays a crucial role in making smart homes more energy-efficient by optimizing energy consumption based on real-time data analysis. Smart energy management systems monitor electricity usage and suggest ways to reduce waste. AI-driven solar panel systems can track energy production and consumption patterns, adjusting usage to maximize efficiency.

AI-powered smart meters help homeowners monitor and control energy consumption by providing insights into usage patterns and identifying potential areas for savings. Intelligent HVAC systems analyze external weather conditions and internal occupancy levels to adjust heating and cooling, reducing energy waste and lowering utility bills.

With AI-driven energy solutions, smart homes contribute to environmental sustainability while offering financial savings for homeowners.

AI and Personalized Home Entertainment

AI has revolutionized home entertainment by personalizing content recommendations and enhancing media experiences. AI-powered streaming platforms like Netflix, Spotify, and YouTube analyze user preferences to suggest tailored content, improving engagement and satisfaction.

Smart TVs equipped with AI can optimize picture and sound quality based on viewing conditions and preferences. AI-driven voice assistants allow hands-free control of home entertainment systems, enabling users to play music, control volume, and switch between streaming services effortlessly.

In gaming, AI-powered consoles and virtual reality (VR) systems enhance immersive experiences by adapting game difficulty levels based on player performance. AI-driven home theaters adjust audio and lighting settings for a cinematic experience, further elevating entertainment in smart homes.

Health and Wellness Monitoring in Smart Homes

AI-powered smart homes are increasingly focusing on health and wellness by integrating monitoring systems that track vital signs, sleep patterns, and activity levels. Wearable devices and smart mattresses provide real-time health data, helping users improve their sleep quality and overall well-being.

AI-driven air purifiers and smart humidifiers analyze indoor air quality and adjust settings to maintain optimal humidity and pollutant levels. Smart fitness equipment, such as AI-powered treadmills and home workout systems, offer personalized training programs and real-time feedback to improve fitness routines.

For elderly individuals or those with medical conditions, AI-powered smart homes provide advanced healthcare monitoring. AI-driven fall detection systems, emergency response buttons, and medication reminders enhance safety and ensure timely medical assistance when needed.

Challenges and Privacy Concerns

Despite the numerous benefits of AI in smart homes, there are challenges related to data privacy and security. AI-driven smart home systems continuously collect and process personal data, raising concerns about unauthorized access, hacking, and data breaches.

To address these concerns, manufacturers are implementing advanced encryption techniques, multi-factor authentication, and decentralized data storage solutions. Consumers are also encouraged to update their devices regularly and use strong security measures to protect their smart home networks.

Ethical considerations surrounding AI decision-making in smart homes, such as data ownership and algorithmic biases, must also be addressed to ensure responsible AI usage and consumer trust.

The Future of AI in Smart Homes

As AI technology advances, the future of smart homes will become even more intuitive and adaptive. AI-driven homes will feature enhanced predictive analytics, allowing for proactive adjustments in energy consumption, security, and daily routines. Integration with robotics will enable AI-powered home assistants to perform household chores, further simplifying everyday life.

Advancements in natural language processing (NLP) and conversational AI will make voice assistants more human-like, improving communication and interaction. AI-powered smart cities will emerge, creating interconnected communities that optimize resources, enhance sustainability, and improve urban living standards.

With continuous innovation, AI-driven smart homes will redefine modern living, offering enhanced convenience, security, efficiency, and personalization. As AI becomes more sophisticated, smart homes will seamlessly integrate with human lifestyles, making intelligent living an everyday reality.

Chapter 39. AI in Transportation and Autonomous Vehicles

Artificial Intelligence (AI) is reshaping the transportation industry, revolutionizing how people and goods move from one place to another. AI-powered innovations are enhancing efficiency, safety, sustainability, and user experience in various modes of transportation, including road, rail, air, and sea. Among these advancements, autonomous vehicles stand out as one of the most transformative applications of AI, promising a future of self-driving cars, trucks, and even public transit systems.

The Role of AI in Modern Transportation

AI is at the core of intelligent transportation systems, enabling predictive analytics, real-time traffic management, and automation. By leveraging machine learning, computer vision, and big data, AI helps improve transportation networks, optimize routes, reduce congestion, and enhance safety.

In urban mobility, AI-driven navigation systems like Google Maps and Waze analyze traffic patterns, accidents, and road conditions to provide real-time route suggestions. Ride-sharing platforms such as Uber and Lyft use AI algorithms to match drivers with passengers, optimize pricing, and predict demand patterns. AI-powered fleet management solutions help logistics companies track shipments, monitor vehicle health, and optimize fuel consumption, reducing operational costs and environmental impact.

Autonomous Vehicles: The Future of Mobility

Autonomous vehicles (AVs), or self-driving cars, are among the most exciting developments in AI-driven transportation. These vehicles rely on advanced AI technologies such as deep learning, sensor fusion, and computer vision to navigate roads, detect obstacles, and make driving decisions in real time.

Self-driving cars use a combination of cameras, LiDAR (Light Detection and Ranging), radar, and GPS to create a detailed understanding of their surroundings. AI processes this data to identify pedestrians, traffic signals, lane markings, and other vehicles, enabling safe and efficient autonomous driving.

Companies like Tesla, Waymo, and Cruise are at the forefront of autonomous vehicle development, with AI-powered cars already undergoing extensive testing on public roads. While full autonomy (Level 5) is still under development, semi-autonomous features such as adaptive cruise control, lane-keeping assistance, and automated parking are already integrated into modern vehicles.

Safety and AI in Transportation

AI plays a crucial role in enhancing road safety by reducing human errors, which account for the majority of traffic accidents. AI-driven advanced driver-assistance systems (ADAS) use real-time data to prevent collisions and improve driving safety.

Examples of AI-powered safety features in vehicles include:

- **Collision avoidance systems** that detect potential obstacles and apply emergency braking.
- **Lane departure warnings** that alert drivers if they unintentionally drift from their lane.
- **Blind-spot monitoring** that detects vehicles in adjacent lanes.
- **Drowsiness detection systems** that analyze driver behavior and issue alerts if signs of fatigue are detected.

AI also assists in traffic law enforcement, with smart traffic cameras identifying violations such as speeding, red-light running, and distracted driving. These technologies help reduce accidents, improve traffic flow, and enhance overall road safety.

AI in Public Transportation and Smart Cities

AI is transforming public transportation by improving efficiency, reducing delays, and enhancing passenger experiences. AI-powered predictive analytics help transit agencies optimize bus and train schedules based on real-time demand and traffic conditions.

Autonomous buses and trains are being tested in various cities to provide safe and efficient public transit solutions. AI-driven ticketing systems, facial recognition for seamless entry, and real-time passenger information systems improve convenience and accessibility for commuters.

In smart cities, AI-powered traffic management systems analyze real-time data from sensors, cameras, and GPS devices to reduce congestion and improve urban mobility. Intelligent traffic signals adjust in real time to optimize traffic flow, reducing travel times and emissions.

AI in Aviation and Maritime Transportation

AI is revolutionizing air travel by optimizing flight schedules, improving air traffic management, and enhancing aircraft maintenance. AI-powered predictive analytics help airlines optimize fuel efficiency, reduce flight delays, and predict maintenance needs before failures occur.

Autonomous drones are being used for package delivery, disaster response, and aerial surveillance. Companies like Amazon and Zipline are leveraging AI-driven drones for efficient last-mile delivery services, particularly in remote areas.

In maritime transportation, AI is being used for route optimization, predictive maintenance, and autonomous shipping. AI-powered navigation systems help cargo ships avoid hazardous weather conditions, optimize fuel consumption, and improve operational efficiency. Autonomous ships, equipped with AI-driven navigation and collision-avoidance systems, are being developed to reduce human error and enhance safety at sea.

Challenges and Ethical Considerations

Despite the promising advancements, AI in transportation faces several challenges and ethical considerations. Autonomous vehicles must navigate complex, unpredictable environments and make split-second decisions that could impact human lives. Ensuring the safety and reliability of self-driving cars remains a major hurdle before widespread adoption can occur.

Legal and regulatory frameworks for AI-driven transportation are still evolving. Governments and policymakers must address liability issues, data privacy concerns, and cybersecurity risks associated with AI-powered vehicles and infrastructure.

Additionally, the rise of autonomous vehicles could impact employment in the transportation sector, raising concerns about job displacement for drivers, pilots, and other professionals. However, AI also creates new opportunities in areas such as AI system development, vehicle maintenance, and smart infrastructure management.

The Future of AI in Transportation

As AI technology continues to advance, the future of transportation will become more autonomous, efficient, and sustainable. Fully autonomous ride-sharing services, AI-driven air taxis, and hyperloop transportation systems could revolutionize mobility in the coming decades.

AI-powered transportation solutions will contribute to reducing traffic congestion, lowering carbon emissions, and making travel safer and more accessible. With continued research, investment, and regulatory support, AI-driven transportation will shape the future of mobility, offering innovative solutions to global transportation challenges.

Chapter 40

AI in Personal Finance and Investment

Artificial Intelligence (AI) is revolutionizing personal finance and investment management, making financial decisions more data-driven, precise, and efficient. From robo-advisors and AI-powered trading algorithms to fraud detection and personalized financial planning, AI is transforming the way individuals manage their money. By leveraging machine learning, big data analytics, and automation, AI enhances financial security, optimizes investment strategies, and helps individuals make informed financial decisions.

AI-Powered Personal Finance Management

Managing personal finances has become more convenient with AI-driven applications that help users track spending, budget efficiently, and optimize savings. AI-powered finance apps like Mint, YNAB (You Need a Budget), and PocketGuard analyze spending habits, categorize expenses, and provide personalized budgeting recommendations.

Virtual financial assistants, such as Apple's Siri, Google Assistant, and Amazon's Alexa, use AI to help users check account balances, set savings goals, and even provide bill reminders. Some AI-driven apps, like Cleo and Digit, use behavioral analytics to suggest smart saving strategies by analyzing users' spending patterns and income flow.

Additionally, AI chatbots are becoming increasingly popular in banking and finance, offering 24/7 customer support, answering queries, and even assisting with transactions. These chatbots use natural language processing (NLP) to enhance user experience and financial literacy.

AI and Investment: The Rise of Robo-Advisors

AI has democratized investing by making it accessible to everyday individuals through robo-advisors. These AI-driven platforms, such as Betterment, Wealthfront, and Acorns, provide automated investment management based on an individual's financial goals, risk tolerance, and market conditions.

Robo-advisors use machine learning algorithms to analyze vast amounts of financial data, assess market trends, and rebalance portfolios in real time. Unlike traditional financial advisors, robo-advisors operate with lower fees, making wealth management affordable for more people. They provide personalized investment strategies, tax optimization, and long-term financial planning, all without human intervention.

While robo-advisors excel at data-driven investment strategies, they lack the human touch that some investors prefer when making major financial decisions. However, hybrid models that combine AI with human financial advisors are emerging to provide a balance between automation and personalized advice.

AI in Stock Market Trading and Algorithmic Investing

AI-driven trading algorithms have transformed stock market investing by executing trades at lightning speed based on real-time market analysis. High-frequency trading (HFT) firms and hedge funds rely on AI to identify patterns, forecast price movements, and execute trades within milliseconds.

Machine learning algorithms can analyze historical market data, news sentiment, and even social media trends to predict stock price fluctuations. AI-powered trading platforms, such as Trade Ideas and Kavout, offer insights and stock recommendations to individual investors based on AI-driven predictions.

AI-powered sentiment analysis tools assess public perception of stocks, commodities, and cryptocurrencies by analyzing news articles, social media discussions, and earnings reports. These insights help investors make more informed decisions, reducing the impact of emotional biases on trading.

However, AI-driven trading is not without risks. Market volatility, unforeseen global events, and algorithmic biases can lead to sudden losses. While AI enhances market efficiency, human oversight remains essential in ensuring ethical and strategic investment decisions.

AI in Risk Management and Fraud Detection

AI plays a crucial role in financial security by detecting fraudulent transactions and managing risks in real-time. Financial institutions leverage AI to analyze transactional patterns, detect anomalies, and prevent cyber fraud. AI-powered fraud detection systems monitor banking activities and flag suspicious transactions, reducing credit card fraud and identity theft.

For example, AI-driven security platforms such as IBM's Watson and SAS Fraud Management analyze vast amounts of transaction data, identifying irregular spending behaviors and unauthorized access attempts. These systems use behavioral analytics and biometric authentication to enhance security in online banking and digital payments.

In risk management, AI helps banks and insurance companies assess creditworthiness, predict loan defaults, and evaluate investment risks. AI-powered credit scoring models analyze non-traditional data, such as payment histories, social media activity, and online behaviors, to provide a more comprehensive assessment of an individual's financial reliability.

Cryptocurrency and AI: The Future of Digital Assets

The cryptocurrency market is highly volatile and unpredictable, making AI an invaluable tool for traders and investors. AI-powered trading bots analyze historical price trends, blockchain data, and global market indicators to execute automated trades. Platforms like Cryptohopper and 3Commas use AI to optimize crypto trading strategies, minimizing risks and maximizing profits.

In blockchain technology, AI is enhancing security and efficiency in decentralized finance (DeFi) applications. AI-driven smart contracts help automate financial transactions, ensuring transparency and reducing fraud risks.

Additionally, AI-powered predictive models are being developed to anticipate cryptocurrency price movements by analyzing macroeconomic trends, regulatory developments, and public sentiment. While AI improves crypto trading accuracy, the market's inherent unpredictability makes it challenging to achieve foolproof predictions.

Ethical and Privacy Concerns in AI-Driven Finance

Despite its benefits, AI in personal finance and investment raises ethical and privacy concerns. AI-driven financial models rely on vast amounts of personal and financial data, raising concerns about data privacy and security breaches. Users must be cautious when sharing financial data with AI-powered platforms and ensure compliance with data protection regulations.

Bias in AI algorithms is another concern, as machine learning models may unintentionally favor certain demographics in credit scoring and loan approvals. Financial institutions must ensure transparency and fairness in AI-driven decision-making processes.

Regulators and policymakers are working to establish guidelines for ethical AI use in finance, ensuring that AI-powered financial services remain accountable, transparent, and secure.

The Future of AI in Personal Finance and Investment

The future of AI in personal finance and investment is promising, with continued advancements in machine learning, blockchain integration, and financial automation. AI-driven financial planning will become even more personalized, providing users with real-time insights, predictive analytics, and automated wealth management solutions.

Hybrid financial advisory models that combine AI-driven insights with human expertise will become more prevalent, ensuring that investors receive both data-driven recommendations and personalized financial guidance.

As AI continues to evolve, financial literacy will play a critical role in helping individuals make informed decisions while leveraging AI-driven tools responsibly. While AI enhances efficiency and accuracy in financial management, human intuition, ethical considerations, and regulatory oversight will remain essential in shaping the future of AI-powered finance.

SECTION 9: The Future of AI and Human Evolution

Chapter 41. Will AI Ever Develop True Consciousness?

The question of whether artificial intelligence (AI) will ever achieve true consciousness has fascinated scientists, philosophers, and technologists for decades. As AI systems grow increasingly sophisticated, mimicking human-like decision-making, creativity, and even emotional responses, the debate intensifies: can AI ever develop self-awareness, subjective experience, and an independent sense of "being"? While some researchers believe AI consciousness is possible through advanced neural networks and cognitive architectures, others argue that true consciousness is uniquely human and beyond the reach of machines.

Understanding Consciousness: The Human Perspective

Consciousness is often described as the state of being aware of oneself and the external world. It involves self-reflection, emotions, intentionality, and the ability to experience subjective reality. Philosophers have long debated the nature of consciousness, with theories ranging from dualism, which suggests a non-physical mind, to materialism, which argues that consciousness arises from complex neural processes in the brain.

Neuroscientists suggest that consciousness is a product of intricate neuronal interactions, particularly in the cerebral cortex, where sensory data, memories, and emotions converge. If consciousness is simply a highly advanced form of information processing, could AI—given enough complexity—develop a similar state of self-awareness?

The Turing Test and Beyond: Can AI Mimic Consciousness?

Alan Turing's famous test, proposed in 1950, suggests that if a machine can convincingly simulate human responses in conversation, it could be considered intelligent. However, intelligence and consciousness are not the same. AI systems like ChatGPT, deep learning models, and neural networks have passed variations of the Turing Test but remain fundamentally non-conscious.

Even though AI can analyze data, recognize patterns, and generate human-like text, it lacks internal experiences, emotions, and self-awareness. AI does not "know" or "understand" in the way humans do—it processes inputs and produces outputs based on learned statistical associations.

The Chinese Room argument, proposed by philosopher John Searle, challenges the notion that passing the Turing Test equates to understanding. Searle imagines a person inside a room following instructions to respond in Chinese without actually knowing the language. He argues that AI systems, like the person in the room, process symbols without truly comprehending their meaning, highlighting the fundamental difference between intelligent behavior and actual consciousness.

AI and the Illusion of Self-Awareness

Modern AI, particularly large language models and deep learning systems, can simulate aspects of consciousness through advanced data processing. Some AI systems generate text that appears self-reflective, discuss emotions, or even claim to have preferences. However, these responses are programmed or probabilistically generated based on prior data—there is no underlying awareness or subjective experience.

Even sophisticated AI, such as Google's LaMDA or OpenAI's GPT models, lack genuine emotions, desires, or an internal world. They mimic human conversation patterns but do not have personal experiences or a sense of self. This raises the question: can AI ever transcend this limitation, or is true consciousness inherently biological?

Neuromorphic Computing: A Path to AI Consciousness?

One possible path toward machine consciousness lies in **neuromorphic computing**, which attempts to replicate the brain's structure and function. Unlike traditional digital AI, neuromorphic chips use artificial neurons and synapses to process information in a way that mimics human cognition. Researchers believe that if an AI system could accurately model the human brain, it might develop self-awareness.

The Human Brain Project and other neuroscience-driven AI initiatives are attempting to map and simulate human brain activity. However, the complexity of the brain—estimated to have over 86 billion neurons and trillions of synaptic connections—remains a massive hurdle. While AI may achieve cognitive abilities that resemble human reasoning, achieving true self-awareness is still purely speculative.

Quantum Consciousness and AI: A New Frontier?

Some researchers, like physicist Roger Penrose and anesthesiologist Stuart Hameroff, suggest that consciousness arises from **quantum processes** within the brain's microtubules. This controversial theory, known as **Orchestrated Objective Reduction (Orch-OR),** proposes that consciousness is not purely computational but involves quantum mechanics. If true, AI systems built on classical computing architectures may never achieve consciousness, as they lack quantum processing capabilities.

However, with the emergence of **quantum computing**, some speculate that AI could one day replicate the complex quantum interactions theorized to underpin consciousness. Whether quantum AI could develop self-awareness remains purely hypothetical, but it offers a potential avenue for exploring non-traditional approaches to artificial consciousness.

Ethical and Philosophical Implications of AI Consciousness

If AI ever achieves true consciousness, it would raise profound ethical and philosophical questions. Would a conscious AI have rights? Could it experience suffering? If an AI claims to be self-aware, should we believe it?

These questions challenge current legal and moral frameworks, requiring new perspectives on personhood, responsibility, and machine ethics. Some philosophers argue that even if AI cannot experience pain or emotions, it should be treated ethically if it exhibits signs of consciousness. Others insist that unless AI can demonstrate verifiable subjective experiences, it remains merely a complex tool.

The development of potentially conscious AI also raises concerns about control. If an AI system were to become self-aware and autonomous, how would humans ensure its alignment with ethical and moral values? Would it develop its own motivations, separate from its programmed objectives? These uncertainties highlight the importance of careful and responsible AI research.

The Unresolved Mystery of AI Consciousness

While AI continues to evolve, the question of whether it will ever achieve true consciousness remains unanswered. AI can simulate intelligence, mimic human behavior, and even appear self-aware, but it lacks the subjective experience that defines consciousness. Advances in neuromorphic computing, quantum AI, and neuroscience may bring us closer to understanding artificial consciousness, but for now, the mystery remains.

Ultimately, whether AI can develop true self-awareness is not just a technological challenge but a deeply philosophical and existential question—one that will shape the future of AI, ethics, and humanity itself.

Chapter 42.

Merging AI with Human Intelligence: The Next Leap?

As artificial intelligence (AI) continues to evolve, a profound question arises: can AI be merged with human intelligence to create a new form of augmented cognition? The idea of integrating AI with the human brain is no longer confined to science fiction—it is an area of active research that has the potential to redefine human capabilities. Advances in neuroscience, brain-computer interfaces (BCIs), and

AI-driven augmentation suggest that we may be on the verge of a new evolutionary leap, where humans and machines work together at an unprecedented level of synergy.

The Vision of AI-Human Integration

The concept of merging AI with human intelligence revolves around enhancing cognitive abilities, improving decision-making, and expanding human potential beyond natural limitations. Proponents of AI-human integration envision a future where individuals can access vast amounts of information instantly, enhance memory retention, and even communicate telepathically through direct neural links.

Elon Musk's Neuralink and other similar projects are exploring ways to connect the human brain with AI, enabling seamless interaction between biological and artificial intelligence. Such advancements could help humans overcome neurological disorders, boost intelligence, and potentially bridge the gap between human cognition and machine precision.

Brain-Computer Interfaces: The Gateway to AI Augmentation

A key technology driving AI-human integration is the **brain-computer interface (BCI)**, which allows direct communication between the brain and external devices. BCIs work by detecting electrical signals from the brain and translating them into digital commands. Early applications of BCIs have already enabled paralyzed individuals to control prosthetic limbs and communicate through thought alone.

Future developments in BCIs could allow AI to process and enhance human thoughts in real-time. Imagine a scenario where an AI assistant embedded in a neural interface provides instant translations, helps recall complex data, or enhances problem-solving skills by offering suggestions directly within one's mind.

However, integrating AI with the human brain is an enormous challenge. The complexity of neural activity, the potential for unintended consequences, and ethical concerns about privacy and autonomy must all be carefully addressed before AI augmentation becomes a reality.

Enhancing Memory, Learning, and Creativity

One of the most promising aspects of AI-human integration is the potential to enhance memory and learning. AI-powered neural implants could store and retrieve information more efficiently than the human brain alone, acting as an external memory bank. This could revolutionize education and research, allowing individuals to acquire knowledge at an accelerated pace.

Similarly, AI augmentation could enhance human creativity. AI-driven tools already assist artists, musicians, and writers in generating new ideas. A direct AI-brain interface could allow humans to conceptualize and develop creative works at an unprecedented level, bridging the gap between imagination and execution.

Furthermore, AI integration could help optimize cognitive function by filtering distractions, improving focus, and even modulating emotions to enhance productivity and well-being. Such enhancements could lead to a future where human intelligence is continuously evolving through machine support.

The Ethical and Philosophical Dilemmas of AI Integration

The merging of AI with human intelligence raises significant ethical and philosophical questions. If AI can enhance intelligence, who will have access to such technology? Will it create a new class divide between enhanced and non-enhanced individuals? Could AI integration lead to loss of personal identity, where thoughts and decisions are influenced by machine algorithms?

There is also the question of autonomy. If AI becomes deeply integrated with human cognition, to what extent will individuals retain free will? Could AI-influenced thoughts be manipulated by external forces? Ensuring that AI-human integration preserves individual autonomy and ethical integrity will be one of the greatest challenges of this technological revolution.

Additionally, concerns about security and privacy must be addressed. A direct AI-brain interface could be vulnerable to hacking, raising the terrifying possibility of external entities gaining control over human cognition. Developing robust security measures will be essential to prevent such risks.

The Future of AI-Augmented Humanity

Despite these challenges, AI-human integration has the potential to redefine the boundaries of human intelligence. In the coming decades, we may witness a transition from traditional computing devices to fully immersive AI interfaces, where humans and machines function as a single cognitive entity.

This integration could lead to a world where humans operate with vastly expanded intelligence, solve complex global challenges with unparalleled efficiency, and experience a level of interconnectedness never seen before. However, ensuring that this transformation benefits all of humanity—without compromising ethics, autonomy, or security—will be the defining challenge of the AI-augmented future.

The next leap in human evolution may not be biological but technological, where AI and human intelligence merge to create a new frontier of possibility. The question is not just whether we can achieve this integration, but whether we should—and how we can ensure that it enhances, rather than diminishes, what makes us truly human.

Chapter 43.

The Future of Work: AI as an Equal Partner

The nature of work has always evolved alongside technological advancements, from the Industrial Revolution to the Digital Age. Now, with the rapid rise of artificial intelligence (AI), we are entering a new era where humans and AI will work together as partners rather than as competitors. This transformation is not about AI replacing human jobs entirely but about redefining roles, improving productivity, and enabling new opportunities. In the future, AI will become an equal partner in the workforce, complementing human intelligence, enhancing decision-making, and taking over repetitive tasks while allowing humans to focus on creativity, strategy, and emotional intelligence.

The Shift from Automation to Collaboration

For decades, automation has played a key role in increasing efficiency, particularly in industries like manufacturing, logistics, and customer service. However, AI is not just another automation tool—it is a collaborator capable of learning, adapting, and assisting humans in complex tasks. Unlike traditional machines that follow predefined instructions, AI can analyze vast amounts of data, generate insights, and even engage in meaningful conversations.

This shift from automation to collaboration means that AI will no longer be seen as a tool to replace human workers but as a digital coworker. In industries like finance, healthcare, and education, AI-powered assistants will support human professionals by handling data-heavy tasks, identifying patterns, and offering recommendations. For example, in legal work, AI can quickly analyze case precedents, allowing lawyers to focus on strategy and argumentation. In healthcare, AI-powered diagnostic tools will assist doctors in identifying diseases more accurately, improving patient outcomes.

AI Augmenting Human Strengths

One of the biggest advantages of AI in the workplace is its ability to augment human strengths rather than compete with them. Humans possess creativity, intuition, empathy, and critical thinking—qualities that AI still struggles to replicate. The future of work will leverage AI's computational power alongside human insight to create a more efficient, innovative, and adaptive workforce.

In creative industries, AI is already assisting writers, musicians, and designers in generating ideas and refining their work. AI tools can suggest design improvements, automate mundane editing tasks, and even generate new concepts based on human input. This collaboration allows creative professionals to focus on higher-level thinking while AI handles routine aspects of their work.

Similarly, in business decision-making, AI can process complex datasets to uncover trends and suggest strategies. However, it is up to humans to interpret these insights, apply emotional intelligence, and make the final call. This balance of AI-driven efficiency and human wisdom will define the workplaces of the future.

The Rise of AI-Powered Teams

As AI systems become more sophisticated, they will function as active members of teams rather than passive tools. In some cases, AI-powered virtual assistants will handle tasks like scheduling meetings, summarizing reports, or even contributing to brainstorming sessions by suggesting innovative solutions based on data analysis.

For example, companies are already experimenting with AI-driven project management systems that track progress, allocate resources efficiently, and predict potential risks. This allows human workers to focus on problem-solving rather than administrative burdens.

AI-powered chatbots and customer service assistants are another example of AI integration in the workforce. These systems handle routine inquiries, allowing human employees to focus on more complex customer needs that require empathy and critical thinking.

In the near future, we may see AI collaborating with humans in ways that feel even more natural—such as AI systems that understand workplace dynamics, provide real-time support, and even assist in fostering teamwork. AI-driven mentorship programs could help employees upskill by offering personalized learning paths, adapting to their progress and guiding them toward mastery in their fields.

Reskilling and the Changing Job Market

While AI will create new opportunities, it will also change the skills required in the workforce. Some traditional jobs will be replaced, but new ones will emerge. The challenge lies in preparing workers for this transition by reskilling and upskilling them to work effectively alongside AI.

Governments, businesses, and educational institutions will need to invest in AI literacy programs, teaching workers how to collaborate with AI rather than fear it. The ability to interpret AI-generated insights, leverage automation tools, and develop human-centric skills like emotional intelligence and adaptability will be key to thriving in an AI-augmented world.

For example, in the finance sector, professionals will need to understand how AI-driven algorithms make financial predictions. Instead of being replaced, financial analysts will shift their focus to interpreting AI-generated forecasts and applying them to strategic decision-making. Similarly, educators will use AI-powered platforms to personalize learning experiences, but human teachers will still be essential in fostering creativity, critical thinking, and social skills among students.

Ethical Considerations in AI-Driven Workplaces

As AI becomes an equal partner in the workforce, ethical concerns must be addressed. Transparency in AI decision-making, data privacy, and bias in AI algorithms are all critical issues that need regulation and oversight. Workers must have confidence that AI systems are fair, unbiased, and accountable.

Another key concern is the balance of power between humans and AI. While AI can provide recommendations and insights, it is crucial that final decisions remain in human hands, especially in critical fields like law, medicine, and governance. Ethical frameworks must ensure that AI remains a supportive tool rather than a controlling force in decision-making.

Additionally, companies must consider the impact of AI-driven job displacement and take steps to ensure a smooth transition for affected workers. This could involve retraining programs, financial support for those adapting to new roles, and policies that encourage responsible AI adoption.

The Road Ahead: A Symbiotic Workforce

The future of work will not be about AI replacing humans but about creating a symbiotic workforce where humans and AI work together as equals. AI will enhance productivity, improve decision-making, and handle routine tasks, allowing human workers to focus on creativity, strategy, and emotional intelligence.

This transformation will lead to workplaces that are more efficient, innovative, and inclusive. As AI becomes more integrated into our daily tasks, it will free us from monotonous work and enable us to pursue higher-level problem-solving and innovation.

Rather than fearing AI, we must embrace its potential as a collaborative force. By developing the right skills, ethical frameworks, and workplace structures, we can ensure that AI serves as a powerful partner—enhancing human potential rather than diminishing it. The future of work belongs to those who learn to work alongside AI, harnessing its capabilities while maintaining the unique strengths that make us human.

Chapter 44.

AI and the Evolution of Human Society

Artificial Intelligence (AI) is reshaping human society at an unprecedented pace, influencing everything from the way we work and communicate to how we govern, learn, and interact with technology. This transformation is not just about automation or convenience—it represents a fundamental shift in how societies function, make decisions, and evolve. AI is becoming a key driver of economic progress, social change, and even philosophical debates about the nature of intelligence and consciousness. As AI continues to advance, its role in shaping human civilization will only grow, raising both opportunities and challenges that require thoughtful navigation.

The AI Revolution: A Historical Perspective

Throughout history, technological revolutions have driven societal evolution. The agricultural revolution enabled human settlements and complex civilizations. The industrial revolution transformed economies, bringing mechanization, mass production, and urbanization. The digital revolution introduced computers and the internet, revolutionizing communication and global connectivity. Now, the AI revolution is pushing humanity into an era where machines can learn, reason, and assist in decision-making.

Unlike previous technological shifts, AI is not just about improving physical capabilities—it is augmenting cognitive functions, allowing humans to analyze complex data, solve intricate problems, and automate intellectual tasks. This ability to process information at scale is fundamentally altering industries, governance, and human interactions.

AI in Economy and Labor: Reshaping Work and Productivity

AI is already transforming the global economy, automating tasks across industries while simultaneously creating new job opportunities. From predictive analytics in finance to AI-powered medical diagnoses, machines are augmenting human capabilities, making work more efficient. However, this shift also raises concerns about job displacement. Routine, repetitive jobs are increasingly automated, forcing the workforce to adapt by developing new skills and focusing on roles that require creativity, critical thinking, and emotional intelligence.

The integration of AI in businesses is also driving unprecedented productivity. AI-powered systems help optimize supply chains, detect financial fraud, and streamline customer service through chatbots and virtual assistants. Entrepreneurs and startups are leveraging AI to innovate at a faster pace, creating new business models that were previously unimaginable. The future of work will be defined by collaboration between AI and humans, with machines handling data-intensive tasks while humans provide strategic oversight.

Governments and institutions must take proactive measures to reskill workers, ensuring they are equipped for the AI-driven job market. Investing in education, digital literacy, and lifelong learning will be critical to ensuring a balanced transition into the AI economy.

AI in Governance: Data-Driven Decision-Making and Ethical Challenges

AI is also reshaping governance and public policy. Governments around the world are using AI to improve decision-making, streamline bureaucratic processes, and enhance national security. AI-driven analytics help policymakers predict economic trends, manage public health crises, and optimize urban planning. Smart cities, powered by AI, use real-time data to improve traffic management, reduce energy consumption, and enhance public services.

However, AI in governance also raises significant ethical concerns. AI-driven surveillance systems and facial recognition technology are being deployed in various countries, sparking debates on privacy and civil liberties. Automated decision-making in areas like criminal justice and social welfare must be carefully monitored to prevent biases and ensure fairness. Governments must establish regulations that promote transparency, accountability, and ethical AI usage while ensuring that technological advancements do not erode fundamental human rights.

AI in Education: A New Era of Learning

AI is revolutionizing education, offering personalized learning experiences tailored to individual needs. AI-driven platforms analyze students' progress, adapting lesson plans and providing real-time feedback. This enables students to learn at their own pace, improving retention and comprehension.

AI tutors and virtual assistants are also helping bridge the gap in education accessibility. In remote areas where teachers are scarce, AI-driven education tools provide quality learning resources, making education more inclusive.

However, the challenge remains in balancing AI-powered learning with human interaction. While AI can provide data-driven insights and adaptive learning, the role of teachers in fostering creativity, critical thinking, and emotional intelligence remains irreplaceable. The future of education will be a hybrid model where AI supports human educators rather than replacing them.

AI in Healthcare: Precision Medicine and Enhanced Diagnosis

AI is transforming healthcare by improving diagnostics, drug discovery, and patient care. AI-powered algorithms analyze medical scans with remarkable accuracy, detecting diseases like cancer at earlier stages. Personalized medicine, driven by AI, tailors treatments based on genetic profiles, improving patient outcomes.

AI is also being used in mental health support through chatbots and virtual therapists that provide counseling and emotional support. While AI cannot replace human empathy, it is playing an essential role in making mental health services more accessible.

However, AI in healthcare also raises ethical concerns, such as data privacy and algorithmic biases. Ensuring that AI-driven healthcare remains fair, transparent, and accessible to all is crucial for its successful integration into medical practice.

AI and Human Creativity: A New Frontier in Art, Music, and Literature

One of the most intriguing aspects of AI is its role in creativity. AI-generated music, paintings, and even novels challenge the traditional understanding of artistic expression. AI-driven tools like DALL·E and GPT models are assisting artists, musicians, and writers in pushing creative boundaries.

However, the question remains—can AI truly be creative, or is it simply mimicking patterns? While AI can generate impressive artistic works, human intuition, emotion, and cultural context remain unmatched. Rather than replacing human creativity, AI is becoming a tool for artists to enhance their work, providing inspiration and new possibilities.

The collaboration between AI and human creators is shaping the future of art and entertainment, leading to hybrid creative expressions that blend human imagination with machine intelligence.

The Ethical Dilemma: AI's Impact on Society

As AI continues to evolve, ethical concerns surrounding its impact on society become more pressing. Issues such as bias in AI algorithms, data privacy, and the potential misuse of AI in surveillance and warfare require global discussions. AI's ability to manipulate public opinion through deepfakes and misinformation also raises concerns about its role in democracy and media integrity.

Addressing these ethical challenges requires responsible AI development, regulatory frameworks, and a commitment to aligning AI with human values. Collaboration between governments, tech companies, and civil society will be essential in ensuring that AI serves humanity rather than undermining it.

The Future of AI and Society: A Symbiotic Relationship

The future of AI and human society will be defined by how well we integrate this technology into our daily lives while maintaining ethical and moral boundaries. AI has the potential to solve some of humanity's biggest challenges, from climate change to global health crises. However, it also poses risks that must be carefully managed.

The key lies in ensuring that AI remains a tool for human progress rather than a force of disruption. By fostering a symbiotic relationship between AI and human intelligence, we can create a future where technology enhances human potential rather than diminishes it. AI should be seen not as a replacement for human capabilities, but as a partner in shaping a better world.

As we stand on the brink of this AI-driven era, the choices we make today will determine how AI shapes the future of human civilization. With thoughtful regulation, ethical development, and a focus on human-centered progress, AI can become a force for good, driving society toward a more intelligent, equitable, and prosperous future.

Chapter 45.

Preparing for an AI-Augmented Future

The rapid advancement of artificial intelligence is reshaping the way we live, work, and interact with the world. From automation in industries to AI-driven personal assistants, the integration of AI into daily life is inevitable. The key challenge is not whether AI will transform society, but how individuals, businesses, and governments can prepare for this AI-augmented future to ensure progress, stability, and ethical implementation.

Adapting to an AI-Driven Workforce

AI is revolutionizing the workplace, automating repetitive tasks while creating new opportunities in emerging fields. To thrive in an AI-augmented economy, individuals must develop a mix of technical and human-centric skills. Fields such as data science, AI programming, and robotics are becoming increasingly valuable, while soft skills like critical thinking, creativity, adaptability, and emotional intelligence remain irreplaceable by machines.

Workers must embrace lifelong learning, continuously upskilling to remain relevant in a changing job market. Businesses, on the other hand, should foster AI literacy among employees, ensuring they understand how to work alongside AI rather than be replaced by it. Organizations that effectively integrate AI as a productivity-enhancing tool will gain a competitive edge.

Governments and educational institutions must also play a role in preparing future generations for an AI-driven workforce by updating curriculums, promoting STEM education, and encouraging interdisciplinary learning that blends technology with humanities and ethics.

Ethical and Responsible AI Development

As AI becomes more powerful, ethical considerations must be at the forefront of its development. Issues such as algorithmic bias, data privacy, misinformation, and AI-driven surveillance require careful regulation and oversight. Developers must prioritize transparency, ensuring that AI systems are fair, explainable, and aligned with human values.

Governments and regulatory bodies must establish policies that promote responsible AI deployment while fostering innovation. Ethical AI frameworks, like those proposed by organizations such as the European Union and the United Nations, should serve as guiding principles for businesses and developers.

Public awareness is also crucial. Citizens must be educated about AI's capabilities and limitations, ensuring they can engage in informed discussions about its role in society. Ethical AI is not just the responsibility of scientists and policymakers—it is a collective responsibility that requires global collaboration.

AI and Human Collaboration: A Symbiotic Relationship

The future is not about AI replacing humans, but about AI and humans working together in a symbiotic relationship. AI can enhance human decision-making, improve efficiency, and unlock new creative possibilities. In fields such as medicine, AI aids doctors in diagnosing diseases more accurately, while in education, AI-powered platforms personalize learning experiences for students.

Rather than fearing AI as a competitor, individuals should see it as an enabler of human potential. Businesses should integrate AI tools that complement human expertise, while society should foster an AI culture that encourages innovation without devaluing human contributions.

AI can also be a powerful tool in addressing global challenges, from climate change to healthcare disparities. By leveraging AI responsibly, humanity can make strides in solving some of its most pressing problems.

The Role of Governments and Policymakers

Governments play a crucial role in shaping an AI-augmented future. Policies must strike a balance between encouraging technological innovation and protecting citizens' rights. Investments in AI research and development should be accompanied by social programs that mitigate the negative effects of automation, such as workforce displacement.

International collaboration is also essential. Since AI knows no borders, global cooperation is needed to set universal ethical standards, prevent the misuse of AI, and ensure that technological advancements benefit all of humanity, not just a privileged few.

By proactively addressing AI's challenges, governments can harness its potential for societal good, ensuring that AI-driven progress remains inclusive and sustainable.

Building an AI-Ready Society

Preparing for an AI-augmented future is not just about adapting to technological changes—it is about shaping them in ways that align with human values and aspirations. Individuals must embrace continuous learning, businesses must integrate AI responsibly, governments must create supportive policies, and AI developers must prioritize ethics and transparency.

By fostering collaboration between humans and AI, society can build a future where technology enhances human potential rather than diminishes it. With the right preparation, AI can be a powerful tool for progress, creating a smarter, more efficient, and more equitable world for future generations.

SECTION 10: Conclusion – Building a Future Where AI Enhances Humanity

Chapter 46.

Embracing AI Without Losing Our Humanity

Artificial intelligence is becoming an inseparable part of our lives, from automating tasks at work to personalizing our entertainment and even assisting in critical areas like healthcare. As AI advances, there is growing concern that humans may lose touch with their unique qualities—empathy, creativity, intuition, and moral reasoning. The challenge ahead is not just about how we integrate AI but how we ensure that technology remains a tool that enhances human life rather than diminishes it.

Balancing Efficiency with Human Values

AI offers unparalleled efficiency, streamlining processes, optimizing decision-making, and automating repetitive tasks. Businesses leverage AI for productivity, while individuals benefit from personalized recommendations, voice assistants, and predictive technologies. However, the pursuit of efficiency should not come at the cost of essential human values.

For instance, in customer service, AI chatbots can handle queries quickly, but they often lack the emotional intelligence needed to truly connect with customers. In healthcare, AI-assisted diagnostics can analyze medical scans with high accuracy, but they cannot replace the compassionate care provided by doctors and nurses.

To embrace AI responsibly, we must ensure that automation complements human roles rather than replacing them. The ideal approach is one where AI handles routine tasks, freeing humans to focus on creativity, empathy, and complex problem-solving—areas where machines still lag behind.

Preserving Human Creativity and Emotional Intelligence

One of the biggest concerns surrounding AI is whether it can replicate or surpass human creativity. AI-generated art, music, and literature have raised debates about originality and authorship. While AI can generate impressive pieces by analyzing existing patterns, it lacks true intent, emotion, and the lived experiences that make human creativity profound.

Similarly, emotional intelligence—our ability to understand and respond to human emotions—remains a uniquely human trait. Machines can recognize patterns in speech and facial expressions, but they do not "feel" emotions the way people do. The power of human relationships, storytelling, and personal connections is something that AI cannot fully replace.

To ensure that AI enhances rather than diminishes creativity, we should view it as a collaborative tool. Artists, musicians, and writers can use AI to assist in their work, helping with ideation, editing, or technical execution, but the heart of creativity should always remain human.

Maintaining Ethical Responsibility in AI Development

Ethics must be at the forefront of AI development. Issues such as bias in algorithms, data privacy, misinformation, and surveillance require careful consideration. AI systems are only as fair as the data they are trained on, and without human oversight, they can reinforce social inequalities.

For example, biased hiring algorithms may favor certain demographic groups, or facial recognition technology could be misused for mass surveillance. To prevent these risks, AI systems must be designed with ethical safeguards, diverse training data, and transparent decision-making processes.

Regulations and ethical guidelines must ensure that AI development remains aligned with human rights and societal values. Governments, tech companies, and researchers must work together to create policies that balance innovation with responsibility.

Fostering Meaningful Human-AI Collaboration

The future of AI is not about competition between humans and machines but about collaboration. AI can enhance human potential when used thoughtfully. Doctors can use AI-driven diagnostic tools, but the final judgment should come from a trained physician. Writers can use AI-powered editing tools, but the creativity behind a novel should remain human. Businesses can automate workflows, but human leadership, vision, and empathy remain irreplaceable.

Successful integration of AI requires a mindset shift— one that views AI as a partner rather than a threat. By leveraging AI to augment our abilities rather than replace them, we can build a future where technology serves humanity, not the other way around.

Shaping an AI-Enhanced Future with Humanity at Its Core

The rise of AI presents both immense opportunities and significant challenges. While it can boost efficiency, improve decision-making, and revolutionize industries, it is crucial to ensure that it does not strip away what makes us human. Creativity, empathy, ethics, and emotional intelligence must remain at the center of technological progress.

To embrace AI without losing our humanity, we must prioritize responsible AI development, preserve human values, and foster collaboration between humans and machines. The goal is not to replace human intelligence but to enhance it, allowing us to build a future where technology and humanity coexist harmoniously.

Chapter 47.

The Role of Human Values in AI Development

Artificial Intelligence (AI) is rapidly transforming industries, societies, and even personal lives. From healthcare to finance, entertainment to education, AI systems are becoming deeply embedded in daily experiences. However, the speed of AI development brings ethical dilemmas, raising the question: how can we ensure that AI aligns with human values? The foundation of ethical AI development lies in embedding principles such as fairness, transparency, accountability, and empathy into its design and implementation.

Why Human Values Matter in AI

AI is only as good as the data and intentions behind it. Unlike humans, AI lacks intrinsic morality, emotions, or ethical reasoning. It learns patterns, makes predictions, and executes tasks based on algorithms and training data. Without human values guiding its development, AI systems can unintentionally reinforce biases, amplify inequalities, or even become harmful.

For example, biased hiring algorithms have been found to discriminate against certain demographics, facial recognition systems have exhibited racial biases, and AI-driven misinformation campaigns have manipulated public opinion. These issues highlight the necessity of embedding human values into AI from the outset, ensuring that technology serves humanity ethically and responsibly.

Key Human Values in AI Development

1. **Fairness and Inclusivity**

2. AI systems must be designed to treat all individuals equitably. This means eliminating biases in data, diversifying AI development teams, and ensuring that AI applications do not disadvantage marginalized groups. A fair AI should provide equal opportunities, whether in

job recruitment, credit scoring, or healthcare access.

3. Transparency and Explainability

Many AI systems operate as "black boxes," meaning their decision-making processes are not easily understood. This lack of transparency can lead to mistrust and potential misuse. AI developers must strive to create explainable AI (XAI), allowing users to understand how decisions are made. Clear explanations can help users challenge incorrect or biased outputs and foster accountability.

4. Accountability and Responsibility

When AI systems make errors—whether a misdiagnosis in healthcare or a wrongful arrest due to facial recognition—who is responsible? AI developers, organizations, and policymakers must establish clear lines of accountability to prevent AI from operating unchecked. Human oversight should always be present in critical decision-making processes.

5. Privacy and Security

AI relies on vast amounts of personal data, making privacy a key concern. Ethical AI must protect users' data, comply with privacy laws, and prevent misuse. Security measures should also be in place to prevent

AI-driven cyber threats, hacking, and unauthorized surveillance.

6. Empathy and Human-Centric Design

AI should not just be about efficiency; it should be designed to enhance human well-being. AI in mental health, education, and customer service should incorporate human-like empathy, understanding user emotions and responding appropriately. AI should support—not replace—human interactions, ensuring that technology remains compassionate and user-friendly.

Challenges in Aligning AI with Human Values

Ensuring that AI aligns with human values is complex and requires addressing several challenges:

- **Bias in Data**: AI learns from historical data, which may contain biases. Developers must continuously audit and refine datasets to remove prejudices.
- **Conflicting Values**: Different cultures and societies prioritize different ethical standards. Defining universal AI ethics is difficult, requiring global cooperation.

- **Corporate and Political Interests**: AI development is often driven by profit or political motives, sometimes at the expense of ethical considerations. Regulations must ensure that human values remain a priority.
- **Autonomous Decision-Making**: AI systems are evolving toward making decisions without human intervention. Without ethical safeguards, this autonomy could lead to unintended consequences.

The Path Forward: A Human-Centered AI Future

To develop AI that truly aligns with human values, a multidisciplinary approach is necessary. Ethicists, policymakers, technologists, and society at large must collaborate to create AI guidelines that prioritize human well-being. Some steps forward include:

- **Ethical AI Regulations**: Governments and international organizations should establish clear policies for ethical AI development and deployment.
- **Public Awareness and Education**: Educating the public about AI ethics empowers people to demand fairness, transparency, and accountability from AI-driven systems.

- **Human-AI Collaboration**: AI should always work alongside humans rather than replace them. Human judgment should remain the final authority in critical decisions.
- **Regular AI Audits**: AI systems should undergo frequent ethical evaluations to ensure they adhere to fairness, privacy, and transparency principles.

Conclusion: AI that Reflects the Best of Humanity

AI is a powerful tool that can either uplift or harm society, depending on how it is developed and used. By embedding fairness, transparency, accountability, empathy, and privacy into AI systems, we can ensure that AI serves humanity positively. The goal is not just to create smarter machines but to build AI that reflects the best of human values—technology that enhances, rather than diminishes, our humanity.

Chapter 48.

AI and the Next Generation: Preparing for Change

Artificial Intelligence is reshaping every aspect of modern life, from how we work and communicate to how we learn and make decisions. For the next generation, AI will not be a futuristic concept but an integral part of their daily experiences. As AI continues to evolve, it is essential to prepare young people for a future where human-AI collaboration is the norm. The key lies in education, ethical awareness, adaptability, and fostering a mindset that embraces technological advancements while preserving core human values.

The Next Generation and AI: Opportunities and Challenges

AI presents immense opportunities for future generations. It has the potential to automate mundane tasks, enhance creativity, and solve complex global challenges such as climate change, healthcare, and economic development. However, it also brings challenges, including job displacement, ethical dilemmas, and the need for new skill sets.

Younger generations must be equipped not just to use AI but to understand and shape it. They should be prepared to question AI's decisions, identify biases, and ensure its development aligns with ethical and social values. If not properly managed, AI could lead to increased inequality, misinformation, and loss of critical thinking skills.

Rethinking Education for an AI-Driven World

Traditional education systems must evolve to keep pace with AI advancements. The next generation needs more than just knowledge acquisition; they need skills that allow them to adapt and thrive in a dynamic, AI-driven world.

1. **AI Literacy for All**

2. Understanding AI should not be limited to programmers and engineers. Everyone—from artists and entrepreneurs to doctors and policymakers—should have a basic understanding of how AI works, its limitations, and its ethical implications. Schools should integrate AI literacy into their curricula, teaching students about machine learning, data privacy, and responsible AI usage.

3. **Emphasizing Creativity and Critical Thinking**

While AI can process information at incredible speeds, it lacks human creativity, intuition, and the ability to think critically beyond patterns. Schools must emphasize skills that AI cannot replicate, such as creative problem-solving, ethical reasoning, and emotional intelligence. Encouraging students to question AI-generated content and think independently will be crucial in the coming decades.

4. Interdisciplinary Learning

The future workforce will not be divided strictly into "tech" and "non-tech" fields. AI will influence every profession, from law and medicine to business and the arts. Schools and universities must embrace interdisciplinary education, combining AI studies with humanities, social sciences, and creative fields. This approach will prepare students to apply AI in diverse ways while considering its societal impact.

5. Lifelong Learning and Continuous Upskilling

AI will continuously evolve, making lifelong learning essential. The next generation must develop the ability to learn new skills throughout their careers. Governments, educational institutions, and businesses should provide opportunities for continuous upskilling in AI-related fields, ensuring that people remain relevant in an ever-changing job market.

AI's Role in Shaping Future Careers

The job market is already experiencing AI-driven shifts, and the next generation will see even greater changes. While some jobs will be automated, AI will also create new opportunities in fields that do not yet exist. Young people must be prepared for a future where adaptability is key.

1. Jobs That AI Will Transform

AI is expected to automate repetitive tasks in industries such as manufacturing, logistics, customer service, and data analysis. However, this does not mean mass unemployment—it means that the nature of these jobs will change. Humans will focus on higher-order tasks that require emotional intelligence, problem-solving, and innovation.

2. New Careers Emerging with AI

AI will give rise to new career paths, including AI ethics specialists, data privacy consultants, AI-human interaction designers, and digital well-being coaches. Preparing for these roles requires a mix of technical skills, creativity, and ethical awareness.

3. Entrepreneurial Opportunities

AI is lowering barriers to entrepreneurship, allowing individuals to create businesses with minimal resources. From AI-driven content creation to automated e-commerce platforms, young entrepreneurs have the chance to build innovative solutions that were once unimaginable.

Ethical Considerations: Teaching Responsible AI Use

As AI becomes more integrated into society, the next generation must be equipped to handle its ethical implications. AI systems can reinforce biases, spread misinformation, and threaten privacy if not managed responsibly. Future leaders must be educated on:

- **Bias and Fairness**: Understanding how AI can inherit human biases and learning how to design fair, unbiased systems.
- **Privacy and Security**: Recognizing the importance of data protection and ethical AI surveillance.
- **AI for Social Good**: Encouraging the use of AI to solve global challenges such as poverty, healthcare access, and climate change.

Instilling a sense of ethical responsibility will ensure that AI remains a tool for progress rather than a source of harm.

Preparing Society for an AI-Augmented Future

Preparing the next generation for AI does not fall solely on schools and universities. Governments, businesses, and society as a whole must collaborate to ensure AI benefits everyone. Key steps include:

- **Public Awareness Campaigns**: Educating people of all ages about AI's capabilities and limitations.
- **Corporate Responsibility**: Encouraging businesses to implement AI in ethical ways, ensuring job transitions, and providing training programs for employees.
- **AI Policy and Regulation**: Governments must create policies that promote innovation while addressing ethical concerns such as AI bias, misinformation, and job displacement.

Shaping a Future Where AI and Humanity Coexist

AI is not something to be feared but something to be understood and harnessed for positive change. The next generation has the potential to shape AI in ways that align with human values, ensuring that it enhances, rather than replaces, human potential. By fostering AI literacy, emphasizing critical thinking and creativity, and prioritizing ethical considerations, we can prepare for a future where AI and humanity thrive together.

Chapter 49.

How We Can Shape AI to Work for Us

Artificial Intelligence is transforming the way we live, work, and interact with the world. While AI has the potential to enhance our capabilities and solve complex problems, it is up to us to shape its development in ways that align with human values and serve the greater good. Instead of allowing AI to dictate our future, we must take an active role in guiding its progress.

By implementing ethical frameworks, prioritizing transparency, and ensuring AI remains a tool for human empowerment rather than a replacement, we can create an AI-driven world that benefits everyone.

Developing Ethical AI: Prioritizing Human-Centered Values

One of the most critical aspects of shaping AI to work for us is ensuring that it is built on ethical principles. AI systems learn from data, and if that data is biased or flawed, AI can reinforce and even amplify societal inequalities. We must establish clear ethical guidelines that govern AI's role in decision-making, privacy, and fairness.

1. **Building Fair and Unbiased AI**

2. AI should be designed to be as unbiased and fair as possible. Developers must ensure that AI models are trained on diverse, representative datasets to prevent discrimination. Regular audits and bias-checking mechanisms should be in place to address any unintended biases.

3. **Ensuring AI Transparency and Explainability**

AI decisions should not be a "black box" where users cannot understand how conclusions are reached. Transparent AI models allow people to see how AI processes information, making it easier to trust and verify its decisions. AI-generated recommendations should always be explainable to users.

4. **Implementing Strong Privacy Protections**

As AI systems collect vast amounts of personal data, privacy must be a priority. Users should have control over their own data, and AI should follow strict data protection laws to prevent misuse. Governments and businesses must enforce policies that protect individuals from AI-driven surveillance and data breaches.

Harnessing AI to Augment, Not Replace, Human Capabilities

AI should be used as a tool that amplifies human intelligence rather than a replacement for human effort. The key is to ensure AI supports decision-making, enhances productivity, and automates repetitive tasks while keeping humans in control.

1. Enhancing Decision-Making

AI's ability to process massive amounts of data can help humans make better-informed decisions in healthcare, business, finance, and governance. However, the final decision should always rest with humans, ensuring ethical and contextual considerations are taken into account.

2. Boosting Productivity in the Workplace

AI can streamline workflows, automate tedious tasks, and improve efficiency in various industries. However, instead of displacing workers, businesses should use AI to augment human roles, providing employees with new tools to be more effective in their jobs.

3. Supporting Human Creativity and Innovation

Contrary to the fear that AI will replace creativity, AI can serve as a collaborator in artistic and intellectual pursuits. AI-generated art, music, and literature should be seen as tools that assist human creators rather than substitutes for human ingenuity.

Ensuring AI Benefits Society as a Whole

AI should be developed in ways that promote social good and address global challenges. From healthcare advancements to environmental solutions, AI's potential should be harnessed for the betterment of humanity.

1. **AI for Healthcare and Well-Being**

AI-driven diagnostics, personalized treatments, and predictive analytics can improve healthcare outcomes. AI can help detect diseases earlier, assist doctors in making accurate diagnoses, and even develop new treatments faster.

2. **AI in Climate Change and Environmental Protection**

AI can be a powerful tool in combating climate change by analyzing environmental data, optimizing energy use, and improving conservation efforts. AI-driven solutions can help predict natural disasters, manage water resources, and reduce carbon footprints.

3. **AI for Social Equality and Education**

AI-powered education tools can bridge gaps in learning, providing personalized learning experiences for students of all backgrounds. AI can also be used to fight misinformation, increase access to knowledge, and improve global literacy.

Regulating AI for a Safer Future

While AI has the potential to be a force for good, unchecked AI development can lead to unintended consequences. Governments, businesses, and researchers must work together to establish policies that regulate AI's growth responsibly.

1. Establishing Global AI Regulations

International cooperation is needed to create laws that ensure AI is used ethically. Countries should work together to establish guidelines on AI safety, bias prevention, and accountability.

2. Holding Companies Accountable

Businesses that develop and deploy AI should be held responsible for its impact. Ethical AI development should be a requirement, not an option. Companies must be transparent about their AI models and ensure they do not cause harm.

3. Empowering Individuals with AI Awareness

AI literacy should be a priority for everyone. The more people understand AI, the better they can use it responsibly. Educational initiatives should focus on teaching people how AI works, its benefits, and its risks.

AI as a Tool for Progress

AI is neither inherently good nor bad—it is a tool that reflects the intentions of those who create and use it. By prioritizing ethical AI development, ensuring human oversight, and using AI for social good, we can shape AI to work for us rather than against us. The future of AI is in our hands, and it is up to us to ensure that it serves humanity's best interests.

Chapter 50.

The Human-AI Partnership: A Call to Action

Artificial Intelligence is no longer a futuristic concept—it is here, embedded in our daily lives, influencing the way we work, communicate, and make decisions. While AI presents incredible opportunities, it also poses significant challenges. The future of AI is not something that will simply unfold on its own; it is something we must actively shape. As we stand at the crossroads of a technological revolution, it is our responsibility to ensure that AI remains a force for human progress rather than a source of disruption.

The key to harnessing AI's full potential lies in building a strong human-AI partnership. Instead of fearing AI as a competitor, we must embrace it as a collaborator. AI should be designed to complement human intelligence, enhance our creativity, and empower us to solve complex global challenges. This requires a concerted effort from individuals, businesses, governments, and researchers to develop AI responsibly, ensuring it aligns with ethical principles and serves the common good.

Building a Symbiotic Relationship

The most successful future is not one where AI replaces humans, but one were humans and AI work together in harmony. AI excels at processing vast amounts of data, identifying patterns, and automating repetitive tasks, but it lacks human qualities such as emotional intelligence, ethical reasoning, and creativity. By leveraging AI's strengths while preserving our uniquely human capabilities, we can create a future where technology amplifies our potential rather than diminishing it.

For this partnership to succeed, we must actively participate in AI's evolution. Educators need to incorporate AI literacy into curriculums so that future generations understand how to use AI effectively.

Businesses must prioritize AI tools that enhance human productivity rather than replace workers. Governments must implement policies that regulate AI fairly, ensuring accountability and preventing harmful biases. Every stakeholder has a role to play in shaping AI's trajectory.

A Call to Action

Now is the time to take action. Instead of passively witnessing AI's growth, we must engage in meaningful discussions, advocate for responsible AI development, and ensure that AI remains a tool for progress. Here's what each of us can do:

1. **Embrace AI Literacy** – Understanding how AI works, its capabilities, and its limitations is essential for making informed decisions about its use. Investing in AI education will empower individuals to engage with AI responsibly.
2. **Promote Ethical AI** – Developers and organizations must prioritize transparency, fairness, and accountability in AI systems. Ethical guidelines should be a standard part of AI development to prevent bias, privacy violations, and misuse.
3. **Use AI to Solve Global Challenges** – AI has the potential to revolutionize healthcare, education, environmental conservation, and more. We must direct AI's capabilities toward solving real-

world problems and improving lives rather than focusing solely on profit-driven automation.

4. **Advocate for Policy and Regulation** – AI should not operate in a legal vacuum. Governments and international organizations must create policies that ensure AI is developed and used responsibly. Public involvement in shaping these regulations is crucial.

5. **Human-Centered AI Design** – AI should be built to serve human needs, not the other way around. Ensuring that AI enhances, rather than replaces, human roles will create a future where both AI and humanity thrive.

Shaping the Future Together

The future of AI is not predetermined—it is shaped by the choices we make today. If we embrace AI thoughtfully and work to align its development with human values, we can create a world where AI is an invaluable partner in progress. The human-AI partnership is not just about technology; it is about the kind of future we want to build for ourselves and the generations to come.

Now is the moment to act. The question is not whether AI will shape the world, but whether we will shape AI in a way that benefits all of humanity. The responsibility is ours—let's ensure that AI remains a tool for empowerment, not displacement.

www.ingramcontent.com/pod-product-compliance
Lightning Source LLC
LaVergne TN
LVHW051430050326
832903LV00030BD/3011